COUNTING DOWN to Kindergarten

ALA Editions purchases fund advocacy, awareness, and accreditation programs
for library professionals worldwide.

COUNTING DOWN *to* Kindergarten

A Complete Guide
to Creating a School Readiness Program
for Your Community

R. LYNN BAKER

An imprint of the American Library Association

CHICAGO 2015

R. LYNN BAKER is a conference speaker and advocate for early childhood education, early literacy/school readiness programs, and public libraries. As a former preschool and kindergarten teacher, Lynn holds a bachelor of science in interdisciplinary early childhood education and a minor in special education, as well as permanent library certification from the Kentucky Department of Libraries and Archives. In her current role as the Youth Services Specialist at Paul Sawyier Public Library in Frankfort, Kentucky, Lynn has developed school readiness programs and curricula for preschool children, families, and communities. Through the culmination of her education and experiences, Lynn was instrumental in the development of the Kentucky Public Library School Readiness Task Force, also known as READiness Matters, in collaboration with the Kentucky Department for Libraries and Archives. Lynn received her MLIS from San Jose State University. Lynn currently lives in Frankfort, Kentucky, with her husband, Andrew, and their two sons, Thomas and Tyler.

© 2015 by the American Library Association

Extensive effort has gone into ensuring the reliability of the information in this book; however, the publisher makes no warranty, express or implied, with respect to the material contained herein.

ISBN: 978-0-8389-1333-8 (paper)

Library of Congress Cataloging-in-Publication Data
Baker, R. Lynn.
    Counting down to kindergarten : a complete guide to creating a school readiness program for your community / R. Lynn Baker.
        pages   cm
    Includes bibliographical references and index.
    ISBN 978-0-8389-1333-8 (print : alk. paper) 1. Libraries and preschool children—United States. 2. Children's libraries—Activity programs—United States. 3. Readiness for school—United States. I. Title.
Z718.2.U6B36 2015
027.62'5—dc23   2015005573

Cover design by Krista Joy Johnson. Cover illustration © suerz/Shutterstock, Inc. Composition by Kim Thornton in the Trend, Boucherie Cursive, Source Sans, and Minion Pro typefaces.

♾ This paper meets the requirements of ANSI/NISO Z39.48–1992 (Permanence of Paper).

Printed in the United States of America

19 18 17 16 15   5 4 3 2 1

Contents

Foreword

WOW! WHAT A CONTRIBUTION TO THE BODY OF LITerature around the public library's role in the community in supporting early literacy and school readiness through parent education. Here we see the precepts and teachings of both the first and second editions of Every Child Ready to Read enriched—not only to help parents understand the connection between activities and later reading, but also to give specific examples and advice, bringing your public library to the forefront in the realm of early childhood education.

As public libraries have moved more intentionally in this direction, I have become concerned that, in some cases, the joy of reading and the love of books and reading are taking a backseat to the early literacy focus. In some library systems, there is a move to call storytimes "classes." I am happy to see that Lynn is making a distinction between storytimes and Countdown to Kindergarten storyhours. With storytimes, the impetus for our choices is based on the quality of the books and other materials, our joy in them, and their appropriateness for the ages/stages of the children targeted in the storytime. The Countdown storyhours have the adults' understanding of early literacy and school readiness as the primary focus while using enjoyable books, materials, and activities that support the skills, practices, and domains being addressed.

It may seem daunting to raise the level at which your library provides school readiness support to families and to increase the visibility of that aspect of library service in your community. As we add to our knowledge about early literacy and school readiness—and incorporate intentionality into our programs, services, marketing, outreach and initiatives—we must acknowledge what we already do know while continuing to increase our knowledge about child development and early literacy. This is an ongoing process. Recognize what you do know and grow from there. Our special contribution to the early childhood community is our knowledge of children's literature and language activities and its connection to young children at different ages and stages, the collections we offer access to, and the community resources we offer.

While both formal and informal learning have critical places in a person's total learning, the public library must embrace its education role in the community as the place for informal learning. This is the niche where we make the most valuable contribution, where participants need not feel intimidated, where no one is tested, where no one is judged, where all are welcome, where all can grow and learn. Lynn's tone, programs, techniques, and advocacy approach all support the public library's contribution to informal learning.

Lynn has brought to the public library realm her strong background as a preschool and kindergarten teacher, enriching the community and the state of Kentucky in her role as early childhood advocate.

May this book serve as inspiration to expand what you are already doing or to take a first step in an exciting journey to help your public library play a key role in helping every child enter school ready to learn.

SAROJ GHOTING
Early Childhood Literacy Consultant
www.earlylit.net

Coauthor of *STEP into Storytime: Using StoryTime Effective Practice to Strengthen the Development of Newborns to Five-Year-Olds* and *Storytimes for Everyone! Developing Young Children's Language and Literacy*

Acknowledgments

THROUGHOUT THE WRITING OF THIS BOOK, THERE HAVE been many fellow librarians and literacy professionals who have graciously taken the time to share their experiences with me.

A special thank you to Saroj Ghoting for all the ways you have served young children and families—in your own community and state, as well as throughout the global community. Your work in early literacy and school readiness have advanced the programs and services offered by public libraries today. You have taught us the importance of being intentional. Your support and encouragement has meant a lot to me, and I sincerely appreciate you introducing me to ALA Editions.

Jamie Santoro, thank you for your guidance through this process and for being so patient with me. I am so appreciative of your support and for navigating me through this new experience.

Kathleen Reif, director of St. Mary's County Library in Maryland, thank you for leading the charge toward establishing public libraries as early childhood and school readiness service providers. Your efforts have inspired the rest of us to advocate for our own library services, and there are more public library school readiness services being developed because of your leadership.

To my coworkers at Paul Sawyier Public Library, thank you for allowing me to be a part of a team who truly cares about serving children and families. I am honored to work alongside each of you. A special thanks to Erinn Conness, the youth services coordinator at PSPL. Thank you for believing in the importance of the Countdown to Kindergarten program. I believe, because of your leadership, that we have helped bridge the gap for many families, classrooms, and children within our community.

Thanks to the kindergarten, preschool, and early care teachers in our community, as well as the parents, caregivers, families, and children who have participated in the Countdown to Kindergarten program. We hope that our program has made a difference in your transition to kindergarten. Thank you for allowing our library to be a part of this special time in your child's life!

Thank you to Heather Dieffenbach and Wayne Onkst at the Kentucky Department for Libraries and Archives. Your immediate openness when I approached you about addressing school readiness is why the READiness Matters task force was formed, and why we have been able be build strong collaborative partnerships across the state. Public libraries in Kentucky are working together because of your support and encouragement. Thanks to each and every member of the READiness Matters task force. Your willingness to work with other libraries to provide better, more intentional services to children and families is a great example to other libraries across the country.

A special thanks to the Kentucky Department of Education and the Governor's Office of Early Childhood. We appreciate your support of public libraries as valuable members of our state's school readiness goals.

Lastly, this book would not be possible without the love, support, and (maybe most of all) patience of my family. Andrew, Thomas, and Tyler, I promise to make up for missed dinners and family time. I appreciate each of you for allowing me to type, for quiet when it was needed, and for understanding when I couldn't go participate in family fun. Andrew, thank you for being my best friend (and for playing the dulcimer). Thomas and Tyler—I can't wait to see what you become passionate about in life. I have no doubt you will help change the world for the better.

Introduction

OVER THE PAST FEW DECADES, RESEARCH HAS SHOWN just how important the early years of a child's development are to later success in school. Most states—in recognition of these important years of development—have established guidelines and indicators of what it looks like for a child to be ready for school. While there are many wonderful early and preschool childhood programs in existence today, unfortunately, not every child has the opportunity to attend a formal preschool program before entering kindergarten. The public library is in the perfect position within the community to help bridge the gap between preschool and kindergarten—not just for families and children, but also for early care and preschool teachers, kindergarten teachers, legislators, and other service providers.

Most public libraries offer early childhood programs for children and families, but the development of a program that is deliberately focused on school readiness skills involves specific and intentional planning on the part of the librarian. This book will walk you through each step of creating a school readiness program that is connected to child development and early literacy skill practices. Beginning with the basics of early childhood development, the literacy practices of Every Child Ready to Read, and commonly adopted domains of school readiness, this book shows you how to successfully combine each of these components into a program that is intentionally focused on preparing children for school.

The basic framework in this book is based on the Countdown to Kindergarten program that I developed for Paul Sawyier Public Library in Frankfort, Kentucky. The program was developed in response to statewide kindergarten entrance scores, which showed that the majority of kindergarten children in Kentucky were entering school not ready to learn. While our library was already offering programs that fostered early literacy skills and modeled literacy practices for parents and caregivers, we made the decision to intentionally develop a school readiness program that connected to the definition of school readiness as established by the Governor's Office of Early Childhood. I was able to combine my education and experience in early childhood education with my experience working in the public library in order to develop the Countdown to Kindergarten program.

I first conducted research on existing school readiness programs and began the planning process in the winter of 2012. By spring 2013, our library launched our first adult/child Countdown to Kindergarten program. We had such great interest and success that we decided to offer an additional summer session for adults and children who had missed the program in the spring. After our first sessions, we made the decision to add a program in the fall for adults to attend without children in order to better connect adult attendees to early childhood community guest speakers. Guest speakers were invited to present information to adult participants during the fall session based on the individual needs of our participants. As of the printing of this book, we have kept this basic timeline for both sessions of the program, and change guest speakers based on each individual group of adults who participate in the fall session of the program.

While our programming timeline works well for our library, it is merely a suggestion to help you plan your own. Base your session timeline and frequency on what is appropriate for your own community. Some libraries may not have the room or ability to sustain a two-part, six-week session. It may work better for your library to offer a onetime program. Whatever your timeline or method, this book is meant to offer you guidelines of the types of things you will want to think about as you plan your school readiness program. Feel free to use the parts of the program that work best for your library and community, and/or adjust the parts that do not fit your needs.

One of the most beneficial collaborative partnerships that our library worked to establish was with our local kindergarten teachers. Working closely with your community's kindergarten teachers can provide valuable information as you prepare to connect your program activities to the specific needs of your community. Planning a meeting with local kindergarten teachers was one of our library's first steps toward creating the Countdown curriculum. As a former preschool and kindergarten teacher, I knew that there were some important pieces of information that kindergarten teachers could provide from the frontline of the classroom that we would not have otherwise. Connecting to early care and preschool teachers in our community was equally helpful to the development of the Countdown program. Meeting with early care/preschool and kindergarten teachers helped us gauge how well the practices of preschool-level programs in our community aligned with the expectations of kindergarten teachers. After meeting with kindergarten teachers, and then later with early care/preschool teachers, it became clear that there was a lack of collaborative partnership opportunities between the two groups. In order to help facilitate communication between preschool and kindergarten teachers, our library has since planned a meeting that will bring the two together.

There are many benefits that your library may find from collaborating with the teachers in your own community. Chapter four of this book, "Public Libraries Bridging the Gap," offers some guidance for building collaborative partnerships with preschool and kindergarten teachers, but there may be other ways that your library may find for your own community. The most important thing is that you make the effort to establish partnerships. As our library heard many times during the process, other organizations may not think of the public library as a school readiness service provider unless you make the effort to reach out.

While our library's Countdown to Kindergarten program offers one framework option, there are other school readiness services that can be incorporated into your own library's early literacy–based programs. There are many ways that your entire statewide library system can become involved. In chapter eight of this book, "Examples of Public Library School Readiness Programs," you will find examples of local and statewide programs. The ideas in this chapter can be used to help you develop a program for individual libraries, or to help libraries from across your state develop a collaborative initiative. The research involved in preparing our library's Countdown program led to the realization that there was not a consistent level of public library school readiness services being offered across the state of Kentucky. This realization led me to approach our state library system about establishing a task force that would work together to address school readiness programming on a statewide level.

As outlined in chapter nine, the task force worked together to promote public library services among other school readiness services in the state of Kentucky. The public library was not at the early childhood legislative table at the time. As members of our task force approached local and statewide legislators and those working in the state's early childhood office, we were pleasantly surprised at the positive response we received. By and large, the sentiment we heard each time we made these connections was, "We never even thought of the public library, but it makes sense!" This experience taught us that public libraries have to be better advocates of the services that we provide. We have not been our own best champions in the past, and we need to understand that a lack of self-advocacy may mean that we are not affording ourselves the opportunity to serve those who most need our services because we are not reaching them. Additionally, we have learned how important it is to fully understand how what we do connects to school readiness and early childhood development as a whole. For this reason, our task force attempts to connect librarians in our state to training opportunities that help develop knowledge and intentionality of school readiness programming. We also work to connect to early childhood organizations and advisory boards on a state level. Through working to build these connections, we have been able to offer ourselves as early literacy experts, and to receive support for our school readiness services. It is my hope that this book will help other local and state library systems do the same.

CHAPTER 1

THE BASICS OF
Early Childhood
DEVELOPMENT

I**N ORDER FOR YOUR SCHOOL READINESS PROGRAM TO HAVE THE** greatest impact, it is important that you have a basic understanding of early childhood development. While this chapter of the book is certainly not inclusive of every early childhood development theory there is, it does provide a foundational overview to help you connect your school readiness program to specific developmental milestones that occur throughout early childhood. If you intentionally connect your program-planning choices to these milestones, your program is more likely to help prepare children, families, and schools within your community for the transition to kindergarten.

There are many child development theories that have evolved over time in response to current research findings. While there are theories that have existed for quite some time about the way that the young mind develops and learning occurs—and we will touch on several of these—the brain development research of the 1990s has made the biggest impact on how we look at early childhood development today. In order to provide services that truly link to where children are and where they need to be before kindergarten, it is imperative that you have a basic understanding of developmental domains and theories, as well as how the brain develops during the preschool years.

Early Childhood Development Theories

Theorists such as Jean Piaget, Erik Erikson, Lev Vygotsky, and Arnold Gesell helped pave the way for today's understanding of early childhood development. While each of these theorists developed very different theories long ago, each theory connects to skills that are important for school readiness today.

Jean Piaget's theory of cognitive development asserts that children move through four different stages during childhood.[1] This theory further suggests that two of these stages occur during early childhood, and that a child must move through each developmental stage before she can truly learn. According to Piaget's theory, children from birth to age two are in the *sensorimotor* stage. In this stage, children learn about the world through movements and sensations. This means that children learn through actively doing—by manipulating the things in the world around them. At age two, according to Piaget's theory, children move into the *preoperational* stage. Children continue to move through this stage until the age of seven. During the preoperational stage, children begin to use words and pictures to represent ideas. This stage coincides with the explosion of language that also occurs during this time, which we will discuss more in-depth later in this chapter.

Erik Erikson's theory of psychological development suggests the idea that children move through various stages in order to form an "ego identity," which changes over time in response to new experiences and gained knowledge.[2] This ego identity, according to Erikson's theory, develops into competencies that form a child's identity over time. This theory concentrates on the impact that the environment has on a child's personality development.

Another theory that focuses on how children learn is Lev Vygotsky's constructivism theory.[3] This theory suggests that children learn through social interaction with others, and that this social interaction, in turn, leads to a child's cognitive development. According to Vygotsky's theory, all learning is social, and modes of communication are based on tools from the child's culture, through language, reading, and writing. This theory focuses on the environment around the child as the primary factor impacting how a child learns.

One of the first early childhood experts to develop a list of "norms" or milestones of early childhood development was Arnold Gesell. Gesell was a well-known pediatrician and believed that the innate nature of maturing has more influence over a child's development than that of the external environment.[4] The modern concept of child development being organized into levels of "ages and stages" stemmed from Gesell's theories and research.

Ages and Stages

There have been several versions of developmental milestones published since the work of Gesell. The term "ages and stages" has become a universal term used by early childhood experts in order to organize milestones. Using Gesell's work as a guideline, there is somewhat general consensus regarding the overall sequence of developmental skills, though age level divisions may vary slightly from source to source. Pediatricians often use some form of an ages-and-stages screening tool in order to assess a child's developmental growth. Many well-known early childhood psychologists and pediatricians have published their own versions of milestones or ages and stages guidelines, as well.

The Ages & Stages Questionnaire (ASQ) screening tool is used to identify areas of strength and developmental need according to milestones.[5] The ASQ asks parents to share observations of their child's behavior across developmental areas. The ASQ is used to identify children who might need early intervention services before a child begins school. Many public library systems have become trained in administering the ASQ and offer this as one of their school readiness services for parents. Before your library offers any type of screening as a service to your community, it is important to acquire the relevant, required training. It is also important that library staff who are trained in using screening tools are familiar with the basics of early childhood development included in this chapter.

Brain Development Research

Arguably, the research that has had the most impact on our understanding of how children develop skills is the brain development research published in the 1990s by the National Research Council and Institute of Medicine.[6] This research provided evidence that a child's development is not solely dependent on the natural course of developmental milestones, nor on the impact of the environment around them, but a combination of the two. This research also provided evidence that the human brain develops at the most rapid rate during the first few years of life. From the time of birth until a child reaches the age of five, the brain forms seven hundred to one thousand new neuron connections per second. From the age of six on, new connections slow down significantly, making the first few years of life before a child reaches kindergarten the optimal time for learning.

Language skills develop at a rapid rate during this time as well, and are directly connected to the language that a child hears in his natural environment. A child learns how to communicate by the interactions around him. When an infant is nurtured, spoken to, and responded to, his cries will develop into babbling, which typically leads to a language explosion of more than two hundred words by the age of two. By age five, a child who has been raised in a language-rich environment will likely speak over two thousand words.[7]

Language and communication development is directly linked to a child's vocabulary and literacy skill development. Understanding how a child's brain develops will help you plan activities that foster language and literacy in your school readiness program. It is equally important that you model practices for parents and caregivers in order for your program to have the most impact. Parents play the most important role in developing learning habits, and they know their children best. Providing guidance and making suggestions for activities that are feasible for parents to do with their children at home will reach beyond the walls of your program room and into the homes of the families you serve.

Early Childhood Developmental Domains

There are five widely accepted domains of early childhood development. These five areas of development are commonly identified within school readiness definitions and used in screening tools that measure a child's development as they enter kindergarten. While some early childhood experts may label these domains a little differently, the following are the most common:

GROSS AND FINE MOTOR (PHYSICAL)

This domain includes large and small muscle movements. Gross motor activities are those that require large movements, such as running, jumping, skipping, and walking. Fine motor activities are those that engage the smaller muscles, such as writing, cutting, gripping, and eye-hand coordinated activities.

SOCIAL-EMOTIONAL

This domain includes a child's ability to learn how to play and get along with others, as well as the child's self-perception and the ability to regulate her own emotions. A child's ability to create bonds with others around her and to relate to the emotions of others are also social-emotional skills.

COGNITIVE

A child's ability to pretend and explore are examples of early childhood cognitive skills, as is a child's ability to understand concepts, such as numbers, colors, letters, and shapes. Cognitive skills include the development of logical and creative thinking.

COMMUNICATIVE (LANGUAGE)

This domain includes a child's ability to listen and communicate through speaking and responding. Developing language skills is strongly associated with literacy skill development. This area also includes a child's ability to communicate through drawing and writing as well as a child's development of auditory communication skills, such as the ability to listen to stories and books.

ADAPTIVE (SELF-HELP)

This domain refers to the child's ability to adapt to new situations and transitions. Adaptive skills relate to the child's ability to care for his own needs, such as taking care of bathroom needs, hanging up a jacket, and making alternative choices when met with obstacles.

These five domains offer a reference point for creating programs and services which foster growth in developmentally appropriate skills. In order to connect each child in your program to each developmental domain, you also need to understand the concept of developmentally appropriate practice.

Developmentally Appropriate Practice

Developmentally appropriate practice (DAP) refers to the foundational belief that activities should align both with typically progressing early childhood milestones and with the individual development of each child. The National Association for the Education of Young Children (NAEYC) officially adopted DAP as a part of its position statement in the late 1980s.[8] Most preschool programs today are built on the principles of developmentally appropriate practice. Unfortunately, not all children will have a formal preschool experience prior to kindergarten. In fact, according to the National Center for Education Statistics, approximately 44 percent of preschool-age children do not attend a formal preschool program.[9] Your school readiness program will likely include many of the children who are within this population. Understanding and applying the concepts of DAP will help you provide services that are beneficial to children who do not have any other formal experience before starting kindergarten.

The core belief underlying DAP is that those who work with preschool children should build relationships with the children and families in their programs in order to understand their abilities and needs. Knowing the children and families in your program should help you set goals that are "challenging and achievable," one of the main objectives of developmentally appropriate practice.[10] While it may seem difficult to develop a relationship in the span of six weeks with every child and family who attends your program, this book provides interactive strategies to help you identify and meet your attendees' needs. Using these strategies, you will be able to help families and children make connections between early childhood experiences and preparing for school.

Connecting Early Childhood Development to School Readiness

This chapter has provided several pieces of early childhood development information. As you prepare your school readiness program, begin with these pieces as your foundational base. In order to create a program that intentionally bridges the gap between early childhood and kindergarten, you must understand why you are doing the things that you are doing in your programs. When you choose books, songs, and activities, do not choose them simply because they are "cute" or entertaining, or fit the overall theme of a program. Ask yourself how each of them relates to developmental theories and domains, brain development research, and developmentally appropriate practice. While you may find that you have already been offering some activities that connect to each of these, there is power and purpose in understanding the connection. When we understand the full impact that our school readiness programs can have for families and children, we become better early childhood advocates within our communities.

Notes

1. Saul McLeod, "Jean Piaget," Simply Psychology, www.simplypsychology.org/piaget.html, 2009, accessed December 2014.

2. Erik H. Erikson, *Childhood and Society* (New York: WW Norton & Company, 1950).

3. L. S. Vygotsky, *Mind in Society: The Development of Higher Psychological Processes* (Cambridge, MA: Harvard University Press, 1978).

4. A. M. Gordon and K. W. Browne, *Beginnings and Beyond: Foundations in Early Childhood* (Belmont, CA: Cengage Learning, 2013).

5. Ages & Stages Questionnaires. "Why Screen?" accessed December 2014, http://agesandstages.com/what-is-asq/why-screen/.

6. Jack P. Shonkoff and Deborah A. Phillips, eds., *From Neurons to Neighborhoods: The Science of Early Childhood Development* (Washington, DC: National Academies Press, 2000).

7. Child Development Institute, "General Developmental Sequence Toddler through Preschool," accessed December 2014, http://childdevelopmentinfo.com/child-development/devsequence/.

8. Carol Copple and Sue Bredekamp, eds., *Developmentally Appropriate Practice in Early Childhood Programs: Serving Children from Birth through Age 8* (Washington, DC: National Association for the Education, 2009).

9. National Center for Education Statistics, "All Levels of Education," *Digest of Education Statistics: 2007*, nces.ed.gov/programs/digest/d07/ch_1.asp.

10. Ibid.

CHAPTER 2

INTRODUCTION TO
Early Literacy

PUBLIC LIBRARIES AS A KEY EARLY LITERACY RESOURCE

WHILE MOST PUBLIC LIBRARIES FOR MANY YEARS have offered preschool programs that foster early literacy and other school readiness skills, the preschool programs we provide are not always viewed as kindergarten readiness services among those in the outside world. One of the main reasons for this lack of universal awareness is the public library's oversight to intentionally advocate for their own programs as school readiness resources. Children who may not attend an early care or preschool classroom setting before entering kindergarten may attend public library programs if they are aware of them. It is important that public libraries are intentional in planning programs that prepare children and families for school, and that we advocate for these programs within our communities and individual states. Public libraries across the nation need to collectively come together and promote the institution as a school readiness service provider. The world will never know about these services if we neglect to share information about them. Establishing the public library as an early literacy resource will go a long way toward proving our relevance locally and nationally.

While preschool programs at the public library address readiness skills through storytime-centered activities, in order for your public library to have the biggest impact as a school readiness service provider in your community, it is important that you establish yourself as a community authority on early literacy services. This means that you must understand why you do each of the things that you do in your programs, and how each activity connects directly to early literacy and school readiness skill development. It also means that you must be able to successfully communicate this information outside the library. There is sometimes a preconceived notion that early childhood programs at the public library are mostly intended for entertainment and social engagement. While a successful library program does incorporate fun activities that foster enjoyment of library services and interaction with others, the foundation of early childhood public library programs should be purposefully built on early literacy development, since this is the library's primary goal.

Early Literacy Skills from Every Child Ready to Read @ your library (ECRR1)

In order for your program to remain grounded in early literacy, your activities should be connected to the six early literacy skills included in the first edition of Every Child Ready to Read @ your library, a parent education program developed through a partnership between the Public Library Association and the Association for Library Services to Children.[1]

The six early literacy skills include:

- **Print awareness,** which begins when children notice printed text in the world around them, such as the words on familiar signs and the words in books. This skill is a child's first step toward literacy. Children who have developed print awareness understand that print has different purposes depending on where it is found, and also understand that words on a page are read in a particular order (left to right and top to bottom). Print awareness includes understanding how a book should be held and how pages should be turned in a specific way in order to continue the story printed on the pages of a book.
- **Vocabulary** refers to a child's ability to connect words to objects, people, and places in the world around them. A child's vocabulary development is directly linked to the language that she hears spoken within her everyday environment. The more words a child hears spoken at home, the better the likelihood that she will develop a large vocabulary. Children who understand the meanings of words and have a larger spoken vocabulary are much more likely to become successful readers later.
- **Narrative skills** include the ability for a child to describe things in sequence, such as a series of events in a story. Children who have developed this skill are also able to process the parts of a story that someone

else is telling and can predict what might come next in the sequence of the story. Narrative skills can be fostered through asking children open-ended questions when reading aloud together (interactive reading).

- **Print motivation** begins when a child is interested in reading books and enjoys being read to. Children who are developing print motivation skills are curious about reading and want to learn to read on their own, too. Nurturing print motivation at a young age increases the likelihood that a child will develop a lifelong love of reading.

- **Phonological awareness** is the knowledge that words are made up of smaller sounds. Children who have developed phonological awareness skills are able to play with the sounds of words. This skill helps children sound out words when they are learning to read. Children with phonological awareness skills are also able to recognize words that rhyme and are able to understand that words can be broken up into parts (syllables). Singing songs and playing sound games are ways to encourage phonological awareness.

- **Letter knowledge** is a child's ability to name each letter of the alphabet. Children with this skill are able to recognize that each letter is different, with a different sound and a different name. Children who have letter knowledge skills are capable of identifying letters by their sounds and understand that these individual sounds work together to create words. Letter knowledge is generally the last skill that a child masters before reading.

Best Practices of Every Child Ready to Read @ your library, Second Edition (ECRR2)

While it is important that you, as a librarian, understand each of the six early literacy skills and how they fit into your early childhood programs, it is also important that you communicate this knowledge to parents and caregivers through everyday language that can be easily understood and applied at home. Parents are a child's first and best teachers. It is important to model and communicate literacy skill practices for parents in all your early childhood programs. The five early literacy practices of the second edition of Every Child Ready to Read @ your library connect to the six early literacy skills of the first edition by providing simple practices that should be part of a family's daily activities.[2]

The five practices of the second edition of Every Child Ready to Read are:

- **Talking.** Language development is an important part of early literacy. Literacy is the ability to understand and communicate through written language. The more words a child hears spoken early in life, the greater the odds he will become a successful reader later. Talking with children also helps build their vocabulary, narrative skills, letter knowledge, and phonological awareness. Parents and caregivers can encourage print awareness and print motivation by talking with their children about books and other printed materials.

- **Singing.** Singing songs offers children the opportunity to play with language. Letter sounds, rhythm, and rhyme are all important parts of singing that help with literacy skill development. Singing usually slows down the speed of spoken language so that individual parts of words can be heard more easily. In this way, singing helps children build phonological awareness skills. Singing also offers children the opportunity to learn new vocabulary and gain narrative skills through repeating lyrics.

- **Reading.** Reading is the most important thing that you can model for parents and children during your early childhood programs. When you read in your programs, make sure to explain to parents the importance of reading to their child every day. Model interactive reading by asking children open-ended questions about the story, and talk about new vocabulary with children as you read. You can also offer parents a list of books to read at home that incorporate each of the six early literacy skills.

- **Writing.** Writing is a skill that you may not think you use much in your programming, but any activity that engages children in making marks on a paper is helping them develop writing skills. Writing is an extension of print awareness and can help children with letter knowledge. Writing activities reinforce the connection between printed letters and words. It is important to offer supplies for children to practice their writing skills during your programs. The first word a child usually writes is his or her own name. Providing name tags and markers for children to write their own names is one simple way you can foster this skill in your program. Activities that offer children the opportunity to draw also promote writing skills.

- **Playing.** You may have heard it said that play is a child's work. Children learn important social, language, and communication skills through play. It is important to incorporate written language into child's play as much as possible. Offer children and parents the opportunity to play together during your programs. Encourage parents to point out written words on labels, signs, and objects during play. Plan activities that give parents and children the chance to read and write during play, such as writing grocery lists in a play-area grocery store center, or writing letters and mailing them in a post office center. Play that promotes reading skills can also be incorporated into group storytime through flannel- or magnet-board stories or through singing games that involve sequence and vocabulary building. Play should be an important part of what you offer in your early childhood programs. Opportunities for children and parents to play together should be created with the intent of encouraging literacy skill development in a fun way. Program play should include activities that nurture print awareness, vocabulary, narrative skills, print motivation, phonological awareness, and letter knowledge. Play is a powerful program tool that should help children build all six early literacy skills.

Intentionality

Most public libraries have been offering early childhood programs for decades, but simply offering such programs is not enough. Effective early literacy and school readiness programs are intentional. It is important for programming staff to have an understanding of the six early literacy skills and five practices of Every Child Ready to Read, as well as a foundational understanding of early childhood development. It is crucial that you recognize the connection between what you are doing in programs and the developmental ages and stages of children. Library programs that have the biggest impact on helping children prepare for school include activities that are tied directly to the developmental skills needed for success in school. This makes it important for the programming librarian to have a complete understanding of early child development. State library organizations can help by sponsoring child development training for librarians in their state.

Another way that your program should be intentional is through your networking with schools, daycares, and teachers. To ensure that your library's school readiness programming connects directly to the needs of the schools in your community, you should make a concentrated effort to collaborate with teachers. As the community's leading authority on literacy, librarians have much to share with early childhood educators, and those working in child development have much to share with librarians. Building collaborative relationships is a powerful tool for serving the community. The public library is positioned within the community as a hub for other early childhood organizations and schools; all early childhood service providers are important to your community's school readiness goals. You can help these organizations come together—and advocate for your library's school readiness programs at the same time—through hosting collaborative meetings between kindergarten and early care/preschool teachers. While many communities have early childhood councils in which members of some of these organizations work together, there is not often a time when members of the childcare, preschool, and kindergarten teaching communities have the opportunity to discuss the transition of children into kindergarten. Hosting a meeting at the library provides an opportunity to share with the early childhood community about the library's school readiness services, while also helping bridge the gap between kindergarten and early care services in a neutral meeting space.

In chapter four, we will cover information concerning ways to collaborate with teachers, early care providers, and early childhood councils within your community, but it is crucial to note here the importance of intentional community collaboration. Working with other early childhood professionals will help you identify the particular skills that are most important for children to be working toward as they prepare to enter kindergarten in your community. This simple collaborative effort will help you prepare programs and services which are truly tied to the school readiness needs of your community.

The most important population that libraries should intentionally promote their school readiness programs to is parents. If the library is to have any impact on preparing children for school, our services must also help parents prepare. If parenting communities are not aware of our early childhood programs, it does little good for libraries to offer them. Your library must do much more than simply promote services to parents who already know about your programs. The population that most needs school readiness services includes those who are not yet patrons of the library at all. It is important for the library to go out and find nonpatrons—to reach them in the places where they live and recreate. Outreach services that offer programs for underserved communities are crucial to helping libraries find nonpatrons. A family who is intimidated to walk through the doors of the public library may be comfortable attending an outreach program held at their apartment complex or at their child's school. The ultimate goal of outreach programs should be to help families feel more comfortable about the library, moving them one step at the time toward the library's front door. Just like in-house programs, your library's early childhood outreach programs should intentionally connect families and children to readiness skills that have been identified as important by national, state, and community standards.

For the public libraries that do not intentionally incorporate early literacy skill practices within early childhood programming, ask yourselves what your intent is in offering programs for young children. If it is just to offer an entertaining program with cute songs, stories, and crafts, you are doing your library and community a disservice. Families can attend cute, entertaining programs anywhere. What will make them choose the public library over other places? In this fluctuating educational, financial, and technological world where public libraries must advocate for their services or risk losing funding, what early childhood services does your library provide that are worthy of funding—and why are they worthy? For those parents of children who do not attend formal early childhood programs before kindergarten—and who have never heard that they are their child's most important teacher—who will tell them before their children get to school? Who will introduce unserved populations of preschool children and families to the importance of reading, and who will bridge the gap between early care providers and kindergarten teachers? The public library truly is in the perfect position in time and place within the community to make a difference for children, families, schools, and communities as kindergarten approaches. Do not let the opportunity to provide valuable school readiness services for your community pass your library by. Research the school readiness needs of your community, know where your library fits within community needs, and be intentional.

Notes

1. Elaine Meyers and Harriet Henderson, "Overview of Every Child Ready to Read @ your library, 1st Edition," Every Child Ready to Read @ your library, accessed January 18, 2015, www.everychildreadytoread.org/project-history %09/overview-every-child-ready-read-your-library%C2%AE-1st-edition.

2. Saroj Ghoting, "The Five Practices and the Early Literacy Components Support Each Other," accessed January 2015, http://static1.squarespace.com/static/ 531bd3f2e4b0a09d95833bfc/t/5488f582e4b0ef80eae3c4a8/1418261890237/ crosswalkheadstart.pdf.

CHAPTER 3

SCHOOL
Readiness

DURING THE 1990s, BRAIN DEVELOPMENT RESEARCH WAS released, providing evidence of how critical the first few years of life are for later growth and development. In the decades since, the importance of early childhood education has increased as a political and educational priority. In 2002, the National Governor's Association (NGA) formed the School Readiness Task Force under the leadership of then Kentucky Governor, Paul Patton. The NGA School Readiness Task Force adopted the National School Readiness Indicators Initiative, a seventeen-state partnership focused on identifying the skills necessary for preparing children for school.[1] The members of the team worked together to determine readiness indicators based on state and national research. The task force suggested that states should use these indicators to collect readiness data over time. The idea behind collecting data was to inform public policy based on the needs within each participating state, as well as to track progress toward specific state goals. In response to the school readiness initiative, national, state, and community early childhood services have become more intentionally focused on activities that foster readiness skills. The NGA School Readiness Task Force published a final report, along with a supplemental piece, *Building the Foundation for Bright Futures: A Governor's Guide to School Readiness.*[2] This publication connects the recommendations made by the NGA Task Force to successful readiness methods and practices put into place by participating states.

While the NGA School Readiness Task Force identified recommendations for states based on important indicators of school readiness, it did not develop a uniform definition of school readiness. Instead, it provided a framework for states to follow based on the collective input from each of the seventeen participating states. The framework suggests that it is not enough to simply look at readying *the child* for school; families, communities, services, and schools need to be equally prepared in order to best prepare for the transition of all children into kindergarten.[3]

While the NGA Task Force's report addresses the importance of community collaboration—and does mention the library as a resource to help parents find information on readiness services—the report does not specifically present public library programs as school readiness services. There are many possible reasons why the public library has not been universally recognized as a school readiness service provider, but the ultimate responsibility lies with the public library—and, again, in our own intentionality and advocacy efforts. In order for public libraries to be taken seriously as school readiness service providers, we need to understand not only how early literacy and child development fit together, but also how our services fit within our own state's definition of school readiness. While each state has its own definition, there are five fundamental domains of readiness that have been identified through years of research and are addressed by individual states' definitions.

The Five Fundamental Domains of School Readiness

Each state's definition of school readiness is based on five common areas that are important to preparing children for school. These areas, known as domains, are important indicators for readiness but are not used to determine whether a child is eligible to enter kindergarten. All children who meet state-specific age requirements are eligible to enroll in kindergarten. Indicators and domains are used simply as a guide to determine the strengths and needs of the child as he or she enters kindergarten. Each of the five domains hold equal weight and overlap with each of the others in order to capture a complete picture of the whole child.[4] While these five domains may differ slightly in wording from state to state, these key areas of development lay the universal foundation for school readiness definitions (see figure 3.1).

APPROACHES TO LEARNING
This domain pertains to a child's interest and enthusiasm for learning; the ability to apply current knowledge and skills to new learning opportunities; and a child's ability to stay on task, even when the task may seem difficult.

FIGURE 3.1

The Five Domains of School Readiness

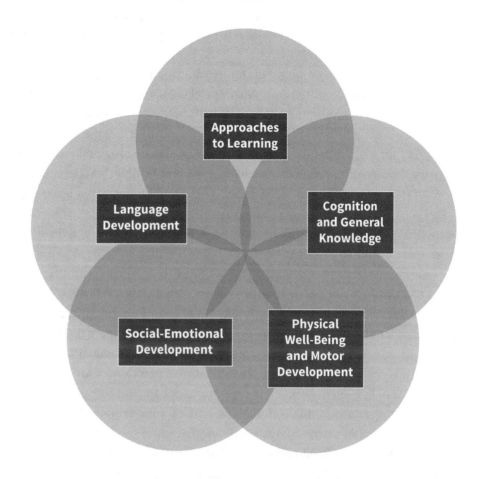

Approaches to Learning

Language Development

Cognition and General Knowledge

Social-Emotional Development

Physical Well-Being and Motor Development

COGNITION AND GENERAL KNOWLEDGE

This domain refers to a child's mathematical reasoning skills, as well as a child's ability to engage in activities that require imaginative thinking. The ability to problem-solve is also included within the realm of this domain.

PHYSICAL WELL-BEING AND MOTOR DEVELOPMENT

This domain refers to a child's level of health and the care that he or she receives. This domain also includes a child's small and large muscle movement abilities.

SOCIAL-EMOTIONAL DEVELOPMENT

Social development refers to a child's ability to interact appropriately with others. *Emotional development* is also included within this domain because the two are interconnected; a child's emotional development is exhibited by his ability to understand his own emotions and relate to the emotions of others around him.

LANGUAGE DEVELOPMENT

This domain is most closely connected to early literacy development. Skills addressed within this domain include vocabulary development and connecting letters with individual sounds. Listening skills (auditory communication) are also addressed within this domain.

While the five domains of kindergarten readiness address important indicators, kindergarten teachers often emphasize social skills as the most important for a successful transition. Listening attentively, working with others, and following directions are among those skills that teachers view as priorities. Self-help skills, or the ability for a child to take care of her own needs, are also skills that many kindergarten teachers emphasize. In order for your public library to best connect to local kindergarten classroom needs, meet with local kindergarten teachers as you plan your school readiness services.

Successful public library school readiness programs combine activities that support each of the five domains with activities linking directly to the needs of the community. Libraries should also reach out to early care and preschool teachers to gain their perspective about skill areas that they see lacking in their classrooms. We will discuss this point further in chapter four, but it is important to note here that many early care providers may not have the opportunity to collaborate with kindergarten teachers—and may not have had much training or education in early literacy and other school readiness practices. Your library can play a key role in helping connect early care/preschool and kindergarten teachers by providing opportunities for training. As part of your school readiness services, your library can offer early care training based on the literacy principles of Every Child Ready to Read and other school readiness practices. Many states have established early childhood–credentialed trainer programs in which public library staff can become certified to offer training for early care organizations seeking continuing education credit.[5] Some states allow trainers to specialize in a particular area, such as early literacy or school readiness.

Why Should Public Libraries Be Involved?

The most obvious answer to the question of why public libraries should be involved in community and statewide school readiness initiatives is that literacy lies at the very core of public library and school readiness services. When early literacy skills are demonstrated and explained to parents and caregivers during programs and services, this provides a real-life example of early literacy activities that can be replicated away from the library. When public libraries model early literacy practices and empower parents and caregivers with information that can be applied at home or in the early care setting, the library is also advocating for itself as a literacy expert within the community.

Whether it is through modeling early literacy practices for parents and children during storyhour programs, providing materials for caregivers and teachers, or providing outreach services to underserved communities, the public library has the potential to reach all areas of the community through services that are free of charge. Families, children, early care facilities, and schools are all eligible to receive public library services, no matter their socioeconomic, cultural, or educational background. This wide-reaching scope of service places the library right at the heart of the community—the perfect place to help children, families, early care providers, schools, and entire communities prepare for the transition to kindergarten. Because the public library is a neutral place that is not formally affiliated with their child's school, parents often feel less pressured as they consider their child's readiness skills through attending programs and gathering information.

In order to best serve the needs of families, again, it is important for public libraries to recognize the parent as the child's first and best teacher. Children begin learning from their parents as soon as they are born, even if parents are not aware that it is happening. School readiness programs at the library should model practices in a way that honors the parent as their child's best teacher while also helping the parent to build their literary practices. Your school readiness program will likely be attended by many parents who are already applying school readiness practices at home, but if you promote your library's program effectively beyond the scope of your regular patrons, you will have parents in your programs who have never heard about the skills that they should work on to help prepare their children. This is where your library plays a part that might not be filled by another community service. As previously mentioned, the public library is a neutral place within the community where anyone can go to find information—and it may be the only place some parents will hear about kindergarten readiness before school begins for their child. Library programs may even be the only practice a preschool child has in a formal group setting before kindergarten. As the primary readiness connection point for these families, it is critical that you provide information and activities that emphasize the five domains of school readiness and the particular skills for readiness identified by kindergarten teachers in your community. Your program also has the ability to empower parents through helping them recognize the impact they have on their child's development.

In order to provide the most intentional services possible, it is important that you understand school readiness information on a state and local level as well, and that you share it with parents. On a local level, the most important relationship that you can establish is a collaborative relationship with area kindergarten teachers. The public library is generally a place where people in the community come to find information. If your library works closely with kindergarten teachers, you will have the best information possible to pass along to parents, including those who the school might not be able to reach. In this way, the library helps to bridge any communication gap that may exist between schools and underserved families in the community. Public libraries should also seek to build collaborative relationships with other early childhood and family services in the community. As previously mentioned, there are many children who do not attend formal early childhood programs. The public library is positioned to provide school readiness services for these families, and should also take the opportunity to connect them to other services in the community.

Why Are Some Public Libraries Not Already Involved?

Some public libraries have been involved with school readiness initiatives within their communities and states for some time now, while other libraries may have been looking for ways to become involved, but are just not sure where to start. One reason that there is not a consistent level of public library involvement lies with the differences that exist in state and local policies. There is sometimes a lack of advocacy on the part of the library, or it may merely be an oversight by school readiness policymakers. The most commonly heard phrase from school readiness policymakers to those of us who have advocated for public libraries as members at the school readiness table is, "Oh! We never thought of the public library . . . but that makes sense!"

Public libraries have changed tremendously over the past few decades; however, it has not been a universal change. Smaller libraries, or those serving more-rural communities, may not have the funding, trained staff, or other resources available to advocate for the library on the same level as larger public libraries or those in more-urban communities. If the public library is going to make a broader impact, it is important that we work together to establish guidelines; that we offer early childhood training feasible for all public library staff; and that well-funded, well-staffed libraries offer assistance through collaboration, mentoring, and training. Building relationships between libraries is essential if we are to make a difference in providing quality school readiness services to our communities.

Another reason many libraries are not already a part of their state or local school readiness initiative may be due to the political climate of their area. Public libraries not only need to do a better job of advocating for their school readiness services, but also must learn to speak the political language of their state and local government. With the shift of political focus to early childhood education, there is an increase in funds available for school readiness programs and services that benefit children and families. If your public library system has not been invited to become a part of community and/or state school readiness advisory boards, you need to make connections that will help establish public library presence. Do not be afraid to approach local advisory board members to share information about your library system's school readiness services. Chances are, they have not heard or thought about libraries being involved. As mentioned, it is vitally important to your cause that you learn how to speak the political language of these groups. This means doing something we as librarians are usually good at: research. If you are not familiar with your community or state's school readiness definition, find it—learn it and make connections between the definition and the services you are providing. Research how literacy goals fit within the school readiness mission of your state. Look into the family framework piece of your state's early childhood initiative. If your state has an office of early childhood, contact them for more information. If your community has an early childhood council (or something comparable), join it.

If you have been working on advocating for school readiness services on a local level, share your efforts with your state-level library system. Statewide school readiness efforts provide the opportunity to work toward standardizing the quality of school readiness programming in libraries across the state, which will go a long way in gaining state-level support of public library school readiness services. There are several state library systems that have successfully become a part of the school readiness landscape in their states. In order to better understand how to get the ball rolling, look to other states who have been down the road already. (See chapter eight for specific local and statewide examples.)

Notes

1. National Governor's Association Task Force on School Readiness, *Building the Foundation for Bright Futures: A Governor's Guide to School Readiness,* (2005), accessed November 15, 2014, www.nga.org/files/live/sites/NGA/files/pdf/0501TASKFORCEREADINESS03.pdf.

2. Ibid.

3. Rhode Island KIDS COUNT, *Getting Ready: Findings from the National School Readiness Indicators Initiative*, February 2005, www.gettingready.org/matriarch/d.asp?PageID=303&PageName2=pdfhold&p=&PageName=Getting+Ready+-+Full+Report%2Epdf.

4. Ibid., 13.

5. Kentucky Partnership for Early Childhood Services, "Kentucky Early Care and Education Trainer's Credential Initial Application Process," accessed November 15, 2014, www.kentuckypartnership.org/Info/ecpro/trainers/tc/tcapp.aspx.

CHAPTER 4

Public Libraries
BRIDGING THE GAP

WHILE EACH SEGMENT OF THE EARLY CHILDHOOD community might be working toward the same goals, if they do not communicate with one another regularly, it is difficult to know. The public library can provide a gateway for improving this communication, which will help build a stronger community of early childhood services. As you begin making plans for how to develop these partnerships, remember to keep the needs of children and families at the forefront of your planning. In order to help families, communities, and schools connect, it is crucial that you reach out beyond the walls of your library. The public library is in the perfect position within the community to bring together families with other early childhood service providers and schools. The public library is also in the perfect position to help other early childhood service providers connect to one another, and to help them connect to kindergarten teachers in the community as well. The first step toward uniting the early childhood community is reaching out to families who are not already receiving services from other early childhood organizations.

Collaborating with Families

There is a large percentage of preschool children who do not attend formal preschool programs, but many of these children do attend public library programs before kindergarten. The public library has an obligation to provide opportunities that these children might not otherwise have before beginning kindergarten. Public library early childhood programs offer opportunities for peer interaction (which helps foster social skills), activities that encourage listening skills in a group setting, and exercises that require the ability to follow directions. This is in addition to program activities which naturally help to foster early literacy skills. Programs should model activities that can be easily recreated through daily experiences at home. Working with families during the planning process before you begin your sessions can help you determine what types of skill practices would be most beneficial to families in your community. Gather this information by creating a focus group of parents/caregivers at the library. Invite those who have children who will be attending your readiness program, and ask those in attendance to share the skill areas that they have the most concern about. After your program has been established for some time, you may even want to ask specific parents to continue to serve on the focus group with new parents. Distribute questionnaires during your focus group meeting, or post a questionnaire online for parents to complete. Use this information to plan your future program activities. The questionnaire in figure 4.1 is provided as a template. You may choose to add your library information and use this questionnaire in its entirety, or edit/add questions to meet the specific needs of your own program.

Meeting with families also gives the library the opportunity to connect them with other service providers, and to gather information from the early childhood community to deliver to families who may not otherwise receive it. Many public preschools and/or other early childhood service providers offer screenings to help identify particular needs before kindergarten. Public libraries can share information about screenings with parents—and public libraries can also offer to host screenings at the library as part of an early childhood program. This provides a public place for screening opportunities, and also helps to promote the library's early childhood programs.

Another way that public libraries can help with screenings is by allowing library staff to become trained and certified in some of the screening tools that are offered in their community, enabling library staff to administer the tool. One such tool that some public libraries are currently administering is the Ages & Stages Questionnaire (ASQ).[1] The ASQ is a developmental screening for children ages one-and-a-half months to five-and-a-half years, which incorporates a questionnaire to be completed by parents. According to the responses supplied by parents on the questionnaire, the ASQ helps to determine if further assessment is needed. In this way, the ASQ uses the parents' expert knowledge of their child to compare a child's developmental abilities to developmental age. Depending on the age of the child when the screening is completed, the tool may also prove helpful to kindergarten teachers as the child enters school. While many states are moving toward administering an entrance screening tool, the ASQ also provides

FIGURE 4.1
Parent School Readiness Questionnaire

Public Library Name

Address
Phone
Website

Thank you for sharing your school readiness concerns with us. We appreciate your time and willingness to help us plan our program around the needs of the children and families in our community. Your responses are anonymous, and will be used to help us develop services which connect your needs to school readiness skill indicators within our state.

1. Do you feel that your child is ready for kindergarten? If not, what areas are you concerned about?

   _____

   _____

   _____

2. Have you and your child ever visited the school where your child will attend kindergarten? Please list the school where your child will most likely attend kindergarten.

   _____

   _____

3. Are there any early childhood professionals that you would like to connect with during our school readiness program? Please list any types of professionals (such as pediatricians, nutritionists, school psychologists, family resource specialists) that you would like to connect with during our program.

   _____

   _____

   _____

(continued)

---

4. How often do you read with your child at home? Does your child have a favorite book or books? If so, please list the title(s).

_____

_____

_____

_____

5. Does your child enjoy music? Please list any favorite songs that you sing together.

_____

_____

_____

6. Does your child attend or has your child attended formal preschool or day-care?

_____

_____

7. Does your child show interest in books/reading? Writing/coloring? Cutting with scissors?

_____

_____

8. Is there any other information you would like to share about your child or know about school readiness?

_____

_____

_____

_____

important information from the parent's perspective. Administering the ASQ and offering physical space for other screenings helps build a relationship between the library and families, as well as a partnership between the library and schools.

Collaborating with Kindergarten Teachers

Establishing a collaborative relationship with kindergarten teachers within your community should be one of your first steps to beginning a school readiness program. Again, in order for your public library to have the greatest impact on preparing children for school, it is essential that you reach out to kindergarten teachers to begin building a collaborative partnership before you offer your program. As mentioned in chapter three, kindergarten teachers have valuable "front-line" information regarding the focus of your program sessions. Teachers observe where each child is developmentally as he or she enters kindergarten; they see the strengths and needs of the children, and also see the needs that are represented by the families of the children who are in their classrooms. In order to plan activities that serve these needs, get input from teachers from each school within your community. Plan a meeting at your library with kindergarten teachers from your community—including all schools, public and private. Ask them to share their observations and concerns with one another, and to share skill areas that are most important for children who are entering their classrooms. Also, ask teachers to share which areas score lowest from entrance screening results in order to match your efforts with fostering skills in these areas. While teachers cannot share individual student scores with you due to confidentiality, they can offer information on what areas need the most improvement overall. Knowing this information will help you plan activities that are the most beneficial to your community.

Developing a collaborative relationship with kindergarten teachers also helps establish buy-in for your program. Your program should be helpful to teachers as you plan activities that will help prepare families and children, and in turn, teachers should be happy to promote your program to families. Ask kindergarten teachers to share information with parents during kindergarten registration, especially if it is scheduled close to the start date of your program. Prepare flyers for teachers to place on tables and offer to attend any special events the school offers during the registration period. By supplying information and being present when possible, you can make personal connections with parents and children while providing assistance to kindergarten teachers.

Everyone benefits from collaborative partnerships. Your school readiness program planning should include reaching out to other early care and preschool programs in your community as well.

Collaborating with Early Care and Preschool Teachers

Early care and preschool teachers can also share information about the readiness skill needs that they observe in their classrooms. For instance, teachers may observe that children need more practice with scissor skills, pencil grip, or turn-taking with peers. Having this information can help you choose skill practice activities to include in your program, and how much time to spend on each one. You should take the information that you gather from early care and preschool teachers and compare it to the information that you gather from kindergarten teachers. You may also want to host a roundtable discussion meeting with early care, preschool, and kindergarten teachers all together. This will give each sector a chance to communicate and share ideas and concerns with one another. A meeting will help provide a complete picture of the developmental levels of children attending formal preschool programs within your community as compared to the skills needed to successfully transition into kindergarten. By hosting this meeting, your library can act as a central link between early care/preschool teachers and kindergarten teachers.

By working with teachers from each level of education, the public library has the opportunity to bridge any gaps that exist. The public library can act as a neutral connector, encouraging discussion and collaboration between early care/preschool and kindergarten teachers. By helping open the lines of communication between teachers, the public library establishes a more streamlined transition for children who are in formal settings prior to kindergarten. When all of the early childhood community is on the same page, everyone involved benefits. The public library is an ideal partner within the community to help make this happen.

Reaching Children Who Do Not Attend Formal Early Care Programs

As noted earlier in this book, a large percentage of children do not attend a formal preschool program prior to kindergarten. It is a real possibility that many participants in your school readiness program will be representative of this population. Again, your program should provide opportunities for these children to engage in hands-on practice of skills that they would not have a chance to engage in otherwise. Locating these children is often difficult; you might not have a specific early childhood organization through which to connect you to them, so use your library's outreach services to connect to families in the locations where they spend their time. This may mean promoting your program through pediatricians' offices, parks and recreation offices, laundromats, churches, and other places where families with young children are each day. You can give out information to families, post flyers on community bulletin boards, or present a storyhour session in these places. It takes research and effort, but it is possible to reach these difficult to find families. Your outreach efforts can make all the difference to the impact of your in-house school readiness program.

Bringing the Early Childhood Community Together

Children and families benefit most from early childhood communities that are united in mission. Many local communities have developed early childhood/ school readiness councils. Public libraries have established membership on these councils within several states and communities (see the examples in chapter eight). However, having such a group is not a universal requirement for all communities or states; nor is public library representation a universal requirement for council/board membership on the state level at this point.

In response to the national focus on early childhood, many state governors have established an office of early childhood within their states. Advisory boards and councils have been formed to offer guidance to state offices of early childhood. In order for public libraries to be seen as essential partners, they must advocate for their place as literacy and school readiness experts on these councils. It is also important that public libraries unite statewide. In addition to creating a unified case for inclusion, there are many other benefits that come from building a collaborative partnership between public libraries across the state.

Collaborating with kindergarten teachers, early care/preschool staff, and families may seem like common sense as you work to develop your school readiness program, but it may not yet have occurred to you to reach out to other public libraries in your state. By collaborating with other libraries, you gain valuable insight into how others serve their early childhood communities. This connection can also open the door to a statewide collaborative effort. As previously mentioned, chapter eight will outline several successful statewide school readiness initiatives, but we will take a moment now to briefly look at a few suggestions for collaborating with other libraries in your area.

1. Approach your state library system concerning your school readiness program or plans, and ask about other public library school readiness programs within the state. The state library may be able to connect you with other libraries that have—or are planning to have—similar programs. Also inquire with the state library about the possibility of creating a committee or task force among library staff in order to promote public library school readiness programs in your state.

2. Once you have established a committee, members can work together to create regional training opportunities and/or regional peer mentoring groups. Mentoring groups should pair libraries that may have more early childhood experience with libraries that have not had the same

level of training or experience. Creating a committee will allow libraries to benefit from shared experiences among public library staff who are working with young children and families.

3. Reach out collectively to your state's legislators. This is an important step to gain support for public libraries as early childhood partners on a statewide level. By making connections with state legislators, you may be able to secure placement on state level committees and advisory boards. If there is a governor's office of early childhood in your state, contact representatives within the office to advocate for public library placement on relevant advisory groups statewide.

While the outcome of your efforts will be largely dependent on the systems that are in place within your state, each of these steps are important to your cause. Public libraries have provided early childhood services for years, but are not universally considered to be school readiness partners. It is worth repeating that in order to make the early childhood community aware of library services, public libraries have to learn to advocate for their own services. The ability to effectively advocate for public libraries as school readiness partners requires that public library representatives are able to speak the language of state legislators—and that they are knowledgeable of school readiness initiatives. As your library looks to develop such a committee, it is crucial to your cause that you choose representatives who have a complete understanding of early childhood public library services, your committee's goals, your state's definition of school readiness, and the principles of early childhood development.

Note

1. See Ages & Stages Questionnaires, http://agesandstages.com.

DEVELOPING
Your Own
READINESS PROGRAM

N CHAPTER FOUR, WE LOOKED AT THE IMPORTANT ROLE COLLABO-ration plays toward building an effective school readiness program for your community. Collaboration can take a variety of forms and can take place between individual libraries, between library systems, and/or with various early childhood service providers. Taking a look at the already existing partnerships that your library has developed can provide a starting point for your program planning. It can also help you to identify beneficial partnership areas that you have not yet developed within your community. Looking to other public libraries and library systems can provide ideas for building some new partnerships within your own community.

In chapter eight, we take a look at specific examples of school readiness programs and partnerships that have already been developed by other public library systems. You may consider reaching out to some of the library systems mentioned in that chapter as you consider how to proceed with your own program planning, or you may choose to reach out to other library systems within your own state that have developed similar successful programs. While not all ideas will work for all libraries, collaborative efforts made between similar programs at multiple libraries can help legitimize the need for such programs.

There are other factors to keep in mind as you look toward planning your school readiness program, including the overall program structure, meeting the

needs of the community, and the best way to align literacy skill practices with school readiness indicators. In this chapter, we will spend some time looking at each of the considerations involved in developing an effective school readiness program for your community.

Considering the Structure of Your Program

There are several structural components that you will want to consider as you begin to develop your program, the first of which is whether your initial sessions will be intended for parents and children to attend together, or if they will be intended only for adults. The main advantage of providing an additional session for adults to attend without children is that your session can better connect community early childhood service providers to the precise concerns of the parents and caregivers who attend. It is more difficult to squeeze guest speakers into the program during adult/child sessions—especially if the children remain in the same room during the time allotted for guest speakers—but it can be done if you do not have the option. (We cover more about sessions for adults and options for accommodating guest speakers in chapter nine.)

Another advantage of offering a separate session for adults is that it offers you the opportunity to work with some of the same families over the course of a full year prior to the child beginning kindergarten (depending on what time of year you offer the session for adults). Again, we cover more of the specifics regarding the actual planning of the session for adults in chapter nine, but in this chapter we take a look at some scheduling options that can enable you to provide two sessions—one for adults and one for children and adults—that will provide services in the fall and spring for families before kindergarten.

Timing Your Programs

Choosing the time of year for your program to begin depends on your intended audience and whether you will offer a session for adults to attend without children. The program that this book is modeled after actually began with sessions for children and adults to attend together in the spring; however, after guest speakers attended the last program with adults and children present, it was apparent that it would be more useful to have an entire session of programs for adults without children. It also became apparent that adding a fall session would add the benefit of working with families longer over the course of a year. The following fall, we added the session for adults, and we were able to provide community resources and host guest speakers based on the specific needs of the families. The program now begins with a fall session for adults and carries over to a spring session for children and adults to attend together. As part of our summer reading program, we offer an additional adult/child program for those families who may be new to the community or may have simply missed out on attending the spring sessions. If your library is able to offer a session in the summer, your program can reach that many more families. We do not require that adults attend the fall session in order to attend the spring session with their child, but we do encourage it when possible.

Number of Sessions

Another scheduling consideration is how many weeks your program will cover. The Countdown to Kindergarten program that this book is modeled after includes two sessions of programs that are each six weeks long. The length and scope of your program should reflect the needs and interests of your community. Smaller libraries—or libraries in communities that are more spread out or rural—may not be able to support a six-week program. These libraries may want to consider starting the process by offering just one adult session in the fall, and one larger adult/child event in the spring or summer. You can still have guests come for the adult session in the fall even if you only offer one session. If your library system is larger and/or your community is more active in your library's programs, you will want to try to stay within the framework of six weeks—any longer, and you may find that you lose families.

Frequency of Sessions

If your library follows the six-week framework, offer one program per week for six weeks. You may want to offer two separate times to choose from—in our case we offer the spring adult/child sessions in the evening and again the following morning, and families choose the session that fits their schedule. The families sign up for the entire six weeks at once, so if they have chosen the evening sessions, for example, those are the sessions they will attend each week. This provides consistency for those in attendance, which helps library staff build a relationship with the families, and also helps families in the program build relationships with the other families attending their sessions. If your library system has branches, each branch should offer its own program, but you may want to stagger when the program sessions are offered at each branch. By staggering when the programs are scheduled to begin, you may be able to accommodate families from other branches who miss the beginning of the sessions at their regular branch.

Program Registration

If you are offering sessions that are six weeks long, it is a good rule of thumb to require registration for the entire six weeks prior to the start of your program. This will enable you to plan each session accordingly. Requiring registration can also offer you the opportunity to gather information from families that will help you plan your sessions. You might want to consider distributing the Parent School Readiness Questionnaire in chapter four (fig. 4.1) as part of the registration process; you can use the responses to help plan the adult sessions as well as adult/child sessions.

Length of Each Session

The length of each program within your six-week session should be consistent. An hour should be plenty of time for adult sessions and adult/child sessions. Adult sessions should have an open format to allow plenty of time for discussion. This helps put adults at ease and allows time for questions and concerns. The session format should be somewhat flexible and change to fit the needs of the speakers each week. The adult/child sessions should begin with the storyhour portion of the program during the first thirty minutes, followed by hands-on family engagement activities during the second thirty minutes. (See the lesson plans in chapter six for more information on these activities.) This helps children and adults get acquainted with you and with the program format, which is similar to what children might experience when they begin school.

Meeting Community Needs

As mentioned earlier, you may want to distribute the parent questionnaire (fig. 4.1) in order to glean information from the families who register for your program. But also consider the needs of other service providers in your community as you plan your program. We have covered several ways that your library can collaborate with the early childhood community, but there are additional ways that you can serve the community through offering training.

As mentioned in chapter three, many states have begun programs in which trainers are certified to train early care providers. Library professionals are perfectly aligned to become certified trainers in the area of language and literacy. While library staff may be able to offer training even if they are not certified trainers, several states require trainers to be certified or credentialed by the state in order for early care providers to receive the required continuing education credit. It is important to research the requirements for your state before offering training. If certification is required for continuing education credit, it would be beneficial to your community—and your library—for a library staff member to become a certified trainer. You may find that many early care providers are intimidated by the recent focus on school readiness. They may feel uninformed or that they lack information about the skills that they should be fostering in their classrooms to prepare children for school. Libraries are well positioned to connect early care providers to resources that further their knowledge of school readiness. In order to best serve those providers' needs, ask how you can help.

Another way that you can link your program to the needs of the community is through screening results. In chapter four, we looked at some of the ways that libraries can be involved with screening scores and/or provide screening. As you develop your program, keep those scores in mind. If language and communication scores are low in your community, target your program activities to those areas. Most library programs naturally foster language and literacy, but again, intentionally planning activities that foster those skills strengthens the impact of your program. Screening scores may also be low in your community in other areas that can easily be incorporated into your program, such as social-emotional skills, self-help skills, motor skills, or general knowledge/cognitive skills.

Connecting to Ongoing Information from Kindergarten Teachers and Schools

In order to stay abreast of the most current information from kindergarten teachers, keep in continual contact with the teachers in your community. Ask kindergarten teachers to send you information to be passed along to families who attend your programs. Conversely, send kindergarten teachers information about the library to share with their students. This level of collaboration helps you establish a reciprocal partnership with teachers, which will provide a more streamlined level of services to the community. Be sure to ask teachers to share any new concerns that they have from year to year. (Staying in contact will also help you stay aware of any turnover or changes in staff over the coming year.) It is a good idea to host an annual meeting with teachers (at the same time each year) in order to review the year and make plans. A suitable time of year to host a meeting might be late summer/early fall, after your library's summer reading program but before the beginning of a new school year.

Choosing Community Guests

There are many different people within your community who would be beneficial to invite as guest speakers to your program. Even if you are still in the pre-planning phase, begin reaching out to members of your community who you may want to invite. If you have already begun a relationship and explained your program to them, when you contact them later, they will be aware of your intentions when you invite them to speak at one of your sessions. Since you will be connecting guest speakers to the specific needs and concerns of the participants who will be attending, wait to actually schedule guests until you have gathered this information, but have guests "on call" when it is time. You may not need every community guest every time you offer the session for adults, but you will need to stay in contact on some level throughout the year. By doing so, you will also establish their buy-in, hopefully gain their recommendation to families, and develop an ongoing partnership.

Community guests can include many different types of early childhood or family service professionals from your community. Below is a list of suggested guests to get you started:

- **Parent representatives.** You may want to invite parents who have attended your school readiness programs in the past and now have children who are attending kindergarten. These parents should be able to communicate what impact the library's program has had on their child's successful transition into kindergarten, and they should also be able to speak about what kindergarten has been like for their child. You may want to consider inviting parents who serve on their school's parent/teacher organization (PTO) or as parent representatives on the site-based decision-making council at area schools. These parents help make decisions about schoolwide procedures and can share about the specific procedures at the school where their child attends.

- **School-based family resource specialists.** These professionals work at specific schools and offer specialized services to families. Their role is to connect families with nonacademic services. This might include such things as helping to provide school supplies for those in need, connecting to nutritional services, or providing assistance to help connect families to the proper channels for securing specific services.

- **School psychologists.** Many school systems have a school psychologist who is responsible for conducting assessments that identify specific student needs. These assessments help with decision-making about special services or placements needed to support student learning.

- **Health department/nutritionists.** Parents/caregivers may have concerns about their child's eating habits—especially as she begins school. County health departments often provide nutritional classes and free assistance with creating healthy eating habits for young children and families. Some schools may also have nutritionists who would be willing to come to your program. Nutritionists often provide services such as hands-on demonstrations for creating healthy meals. Check with your local health department and schools to find a nutritionist, and ask what types of services they might be able to provide.

- **Reading specialists.** Some school systems employ reading specialists who provide additional instruction to students who need extra help. Reading specialists can introduce parents/caregivers to the methods used by schools to help children learn to read. Information presented by reading specialists usually links well with the early literacy skills that your program should be fostering.
- **School nurses.** School nurses can offer information about records needed for kindergarten registration, including immunization records and health physicals. They can also speak to adults about school health procedures, such as giving prescription medication at school, illness protocols, and at-school health services.
- **Speech, occupational, and physical therapists.** You may have parents who have questions about special services for their children. School systems employ therapists who provide specialized services for children who need them. If a parent/caregiver expresses concern or interest in information about these services, invite school-based therapists to attend one of your sessions for adults.
- **Kindergarten teachers.** It is a natural choice to invite kindergarten teachers to your program. You may want to invite several to come to your last adult program to field questions from parents and caregivers through a panel discussion format. You may even decide to invite the children to come to the very last adult session in order to meet the teachers, but it is also helpful to have a session for adults to meet with the teachers without the children in order to provide the opportunity for open discussion. Additionally, invite the kindergarten teachers to attend the last session of the adult/child program. This is a great opportunity to allow the children to get a sneak peek at what they can expect in kindergarten. You may want to incorporate a song or activity from one of the kindergarten classrooms from your community in order to provide something that will be familiar to children when they begin school. As you reach out to kindergarten teachers in your community, ask for a song, fingerplay, rhyme, or other group activity that they are willing to share. Invite the teachers to share information, photos, slide presentations, and/or handouts when they visit. You might also want to invite the teachers to read a book or participate in a song that you have been doing with the children and families in your program. It is important to invite kindergarten teachers from the schools where the children in your program will be attending. Be sure to ask parents/caregivers for this information during the registration process so that you have plenty of time to reach out to the appropriate teachers.

Another type of guest that you may want to consider inviting to your programs has more to do with support of your program, and less to do with what they might actually share with your attendees. These guests may include the principals and superintendents of your community's schools, your city's mayor, local legislators, school board members, and/or your library's board members. Your community's newspaper or news channel can also be invited in order to publicize what your program is providing for the community. It is vital to your community that you establish partnerships in order to build united services for families and children in your community, and it is equally important that you promote your program whenever you are able in order to reach families who can benefit from attending.

Cross-Matching ECRR, School Readiness, and Early Childhood Standards

As you develop your school readiness program, deliberately look for ways to match the best practices of early literacy, indicators of school readiness, and early childhood standards. By developing your program in this way, you will help families and children best prepare for school across multiple areas. Look for ways that your state's early childhood standards and indicators for school readiness align with emergent literacy skills and the five best practices from Every Child Ready to Read.[1] After you have done the work to link each of these together, share the outcomes with early care staff, preschool teachers, and kindergarten teachers in your community. By demonstrating how each of the pieces overlap, your library can educate the early childhood community on the ways that your library programs contribute to school readiness. To get you started on the process of cross-matching between each, this section provides the framework of the original Countdown to Kindergarten program modeled in this book.

CONNECTING EVERY CHILD READY TO READ AND SCHOOL READINESS

The early literacy skills and the best practices of *Every Child Ready to Read* (outlined in chapter two) complement the indicators of school readiness that have been adopted by most states. The five domains of readiness, which are somewhat universal, are detailed in chapter three: approaches to learning; general knowledge; physical well-being; social-emotional development; and language development. While the foundational skills of the Every Child Ready to Read curriculum are naturally centered on literacy development, they also correspond to the five widely adopted domains of school readiness. The table in figure 5.1 demonstrates how early literacy skills, the best practices from ECRR2, and school readiness domains interrelate. This was created during the development of the Countdown to Kindergarten program and used to create the readiness calendar in the chapter seven appendix.

FIGURE 5.1

Cross-Matching ECRR 1 and 2 and School Readiness Domains

ECRR Best Practices	ECRR Early Literacy Skills	School Readiness Domains	Rationale
Talking	• vocabulary • narrative • phonological awareness	• social-emotional development • language development	Talking provides a natural mode for developing new words and sounds, as well as socially connecting with others.
Singing	• vocabulary • narrative • print motivation • phonological awareness	• approaches to learning • social-emotional development • language development	Singing can introduce new words and expand memorization skills; it also slows down sounds. It also allows for socially connecting the group.
Reading	• print awareness • vocabulary • narrative • print motivation • phonological awareness • letter knowledge	• approaches to learning • cognition and general knowledge • language development	Reading together helps introduce the concept of print. New words, concepts, sounds, and information can be learned through the narration of the story.
Writing	• print awareness • vocabulary • narrative • letter knowledge	• cognitive and general knowledge • physical well-being and motor development • language development	Writing and drawing skills connect to the concept that there is meaning in printed text. Learning new words and letters can be supported through writing activities. Writing is developed through growth in fine-motor skills.
Playing	• print awareness • vocabulary • narrative • print motivation	• approaches to learning • cognition and general knowledge • social-emotional development • language development	Printed text that is incorporated into play cultivates the awareness that print has meaning. It also provides the opportunity for children to learn new words and concepts. Playing with peers allows children to develop language and social skills.

Early Childhood Standards

Another resource that was used in the development of the Countdown program was Kentucky's Early Childhood Standards.[2] These standards were revised by the state to align with Kentucky's definition of school readiness developed by the Governor's Office of Early Childhood. The standards outline specific benchmarks that children should be able to demonstrate at each age level (birth through age three and ages three to four) prior to kindergarten. The readiness calendar and the lesson plans in this book used the standards as a guide in combination with early literacy practices and school readiness indicators. This helped ensure that the Countdown to Kindergarten curriculum was focused on producing the same early childhood outcomes of development that are expected at the state level. As you develop your school readiness program, gather information from your state department of education and/or your governor's office of early childhood. Having all of the information that is used in your state to determine school readiness will help you develop a consistent program.

Entrance Screening Tools

Most states have adopted entrance screening tools to help determine each child's level of readiness and need as they enter kindergarten. The scores are used as a starting point for each child, and are not used to prevent a child from entering kindergarten. States have an age requirement for kindergarten registration—this is the only requirement for starting public school. The screening results simply help teachers know what areas need specific focus for each child. The BRIGANCE Early Childhood Kindergarten Screen III is the screening tool used in the state of Kentucky.[3] The BRIGANCE screener corresponds with each of the areas of school readiness indicated within Kentucky's definition of school readiness. The screening tool and state/county results were reviewed as part of the development of the Countdown to Kindergarten program. Reports are provided on a state and local level by the Governor's Office of Early Childhood. These reports helped to identify areas of need in our library's community. The Countdown program used these results to help develop activities which foster skills in the areas with the lowest scores. We did not use specific screening questions or activities in our program—this would not be appropriate, as the goal is not to simply help children answer questions correctly, but to help children develop skills that are generalized across all settings.

While you do not want to intentionally "teach to the test" through your program, it is important that you understand what types of skills are being screened as children enter kindergarten in your state. It is also helpful to understand what areas of the screening tool score lowest in your state and community. Your program activities should address low-scoring skills without using the exact material from the screening tool. As mentioned earlier, your library program will serve children who have no other formal early childhood experience before kindergarten. For this reason, it is crucial that you offer experiences which help grow the needed skills for successful entrance into kindergarten.

The next chapter provides specific lesson plans for a six-week adult/child program based on the original Countdown to Kindergarten program. Use the lesson plans as provided, or as a framework for creating your own. In order to create a program that meets the needs of your community, keep in mind the children and families you will be serving. Connect your lesson plans to the early childhood developmental standards and indicators of readiness as set forth by your state, county, and community. By establishing collaborative partnerships within your community—and by building your program on the foundational early literacy practices of Every Child Ready to Read—your program has the biggest chance for helping children, families, and communities be ready for kindergarten.

Notes

1. Elaine Meyers and Harriet Henderson, "Overview of Every Child Ready to Read @ your library, 1st Edition," Every Child Ready to Read @ your library, accessed January 18, 2015, www.everychildreadytoread.org/project-history%09/overview-every-child-ready-read-your-library%C2%AE-1st-edition.

2. Kentucky Early Childhood Standards, accessed January 18, 2015, http://kidsnow.ky.gov/Improving-Early-Care/Documents/Kentucky%20Early%20Childhood%20Standards.pdf.

3. The BRIGANCE K & 1 Screen III: Kentucky's New Kindergarten Readiness Screener, accessed January 18, 2015, www.curriculumassociates.com/products/brigance-kindergarten-ky.aspx?statecode=KY&source=KENTUCKY.

CHAPTER 6

ADULT-CHILD PROGRAM
Lesson Plans

THIS CHAPTER WILL GUIDE YOU THROUGH A SIX-WEEK school readiness program. The lesson plans included are intended to be used with parents/caregivers and preschool children who will be entering kindergarten at the beginning of the next school year. Ideally, this program should be offered in the spring or summer in order to have the best carryover for children entering kindergarten in the fall. The lesson plans are tied directly to the readiness calendar provided in the chapter seven appendix. The calendar should be printed and given to adults at the close of the first session.

Each week's lesson plan lists an "early literacy practice" from the second edition of Every Child Ready to Read and a "readiness domain focus" for the week. These focus areas are there to intentionally tie each book, song, and activity to developing early literacy and school readiness skills with the children in your sessions. Each week's skill practice and readiness domain focus corresponds with a month of the readiness calendar:

Lesson Plan week 1/Readiness Calendar month 1: **Talking**
Lesson Plan week 2/Readiness Calendar month 2: **Singing**
Lesson Plan week 3/Readiness Calendar month 3: **Reading**
Lesson Plan week 4/Readiness Calendar month 4: **Writing**
Lesson Plan week 5/Readiness Calendar month 5: **Playing**
Lesson Plan week 6/Readiness Calendar month 6: **Self-help/Motor Skills**

Connecting lesson plans to the readiness calendar in this way provides a link between the readiness practices that you might model for adults during program sessions, and the calendar activities for adults and children to do at home.

Each lesson plan includes "adult asides," which provide quick explanations for you to share with the adults attending your program. These asides verbally connect the program activities to school readiness and early literacy practices. This is meant to explain your reasons for including the activities and encourage adults to engage in similar activities at home. Suggestions are also included in the form of notes with some of the activities. These notes include resources to use with the activities, including reproducible patterns, fingerplay movements, further explanations, and links to other resources available online.

Interaction Stations

Each week's lesson plan includes four "interaction stations." These stations are meant to provide a way for adults and children to connect with one another through engaging in specific activities that correspond to that week's Every Child Ready to Read practice and readiness skill focus area. The stations should be set up prior to the program. Some stations require tables, but some may be more appropriate as floor activities. Instructions should be placed at each station, explaining to adults how they should interact with their children and the materials. Instructions may be printed out in the form of a handout, or printed on cardstock folded into a table tent and placed at each station.

Consider your space when setting up the stations in your room. If the space you have does not provide enough room for all the stations, choose one or two that fit the needs of your program and the space that you have. The activities at the stations can also be altered or changed to fit your needs.

It is important that stations are not distracting during the storyhour/group time of your program. If possible, arrange the room so that the stations are away from the group sitting area. If your program space does not allow that, it may mean keeping supplies in closed containers. Additionally, keep the supplies for the stations away from the entrance to the room. As children come in, they may be distracted right away. Starting out on the right foot will establish the flow of the program. Adults and children should be encouraged to move to each station at their own pace and begin at any station they choose.

Program Books

The lesson plans in this chapter include an average of three books per program; some are coupled with songs, fingerplays, or magnet board stories. The books suggested for each program connect to the skill practice and readiness focus each week. If you do not have the suggested books readily available, look for other books that fit the focus area that week. The lesson plans are not thematic in nature—they were not developed around a central concept such as colors, farm animals, or the ocean. While there are instances where concepts are brought into the program, they are not the focus of this program. If you choose to incorporate a theme, that is fine, but it is most important that your readiness programs focus on best practices and skill development. This may mean choosing books, songs, and activities that are seemingly unrelated. That is perfectly acceptable. The point of a readiness program should not be to simply "entertain" participants. Rather, through intentional planning on the part of the program leader, the point of a true school readiness program should be to foster skills that prepare children and families for a successful transition into kindergarten.

LESSON PLAN: WEEK 1

ECRR practice: Talking
Readiness domain focus: Social-emotional development, language development

Introduction to the Program

Introduce yourself to the adults and children in the room. Explain to them that you are going to have a great time working on skills that will help the children get ready for kindergarten. Briefly explain that you will work on a different readiness skill each week.

Introduce the first week's skill: talking. Explain that talking helps children learn new words and also helps them learn social skills, such as taking turns in conversation. Talk about the importance of language at home, and encourage adults to talk with their children often.

The song below is a suggestion. If you have asked kindergarten teachers to share a classroom song for your program, it is acceptable to use that song at the beginning of each session. Explain that you will open the program each week with the same song, and introduce the song to the entire group. When you are finished, encourage everyone to sing the song with you a second time.

Opening Song: "Talk, Sing, Read, Write, Play"
(to the tune of "Goodnight, Ladies")

> Talk, sing, read, write, play,
> Talk, sing, read, write, play,
> Talk, sing, read, write, play,
> Talk, sing, read, write, play.
> *(repeat)*

Book: *Lemons Are Not Red*

by Laura Seeger (Square Fish, Reprint 2006)

Adult aside: "We are going to read a book together that focuses on color concepts. It is important to engage your child when you read books together by asking questions about the pictures as you read. I am going to ask the children to identify colors as we read the book together."

Note: As you read the book, ask the children if the items on the page are the correct color before reading the words on the page. Ask them to tell you what color each item should be before you turn the page.

Song: "Apples Are Red"

(to the tune of "Do You Know the Muffin Man?")

Adult/child aside: "We are going to sing a song about colors. Singing helps slow down the sounds in words, which helps children develop prereading skills. We are also going to work on identifying colors in this song."

> Apples are red,
> Carrots are orange,
> Lemons are yellow,
> Frogs are green.
> The sky is blue.
> Sometimes violet, too.
> And, we know our colors.

Note: Reproduce each of the illustrations on pages 61–66 (figures 6.1 to 6.5) onto colored cardstock that corresponds with the correct color of each individual object. Give out one of the objects to each child, and encourage children to stand up with their object as they hear their object in the song.

Book/magnet story: *Mouse Paint*

by Ellen Stoll Walsh (HMH Books for Young Readers, 1995)

Movement/song: "What Color Are You Wearing?"

by The Kiboomers (from Top 30 Kindergarten Songs, Kiboomu, 2014)

Book: *Brown Bear, Brown Bear, What Do You See?*

by Bill Martin Jr. (illus. by Eric Carle; Henry Holt and Company, 1967)

Interaction Stations

Adult/child aside: Explain that adults and children will work together at interaction stations at the end of the program each week. Explain that there will be several different stations around the room with instructions for completing different activities. Emphasize the importance of adults interacting with the children at each station before directing the group to the stations.

1. **Color matching game:** Write or type the following descriptions on small cardstock. Encourage adults to read the description cards and ask their child to name the items that are described after they finish reading all the words of each description. This fosters turn taking skills, which helps children learn the skills necessary for conversation.

   Description: It's crunchy, red, shiny, and grows on a tree. *(an apple)*

   Description: It's juicy, orange, and you squeeze it to make juice. *(an orange)*

   Description: It's big, round, is in the sky, and is yellow. *(the sun)*

   Description: It grows in the yard, has to be cut, and is green. *(grass)*

   Description: It is something over our heads that is usually blue in the daytime. *(the sky)*

   Description: They are a kind of fruit that is small and round. They can be purple, green, or red. *(grapes)*

2. **Retelling the story:** Provide plastic echo microphones with a copy of *Brown Bear, Brown Bear* by Bill Martin Jr. and illustrated by Eric Carle. Encourage adults to read the words "Brown bear, brown bear, what do you see?" Children should answer by speaking the phrase that describes each of the animals into the echo microphone.

3. **Puppet stage:** Provide puppets and a stage area where children can act out a story. In your instructions, encourage adults to act as the audience as their children use the puppets to tell a story at this station.

4. **Craft—puppets:** Supply precut paper puppets using the pattern at the end of this chapter (figure 6.6). Enlarge the pattern on a copier as needed. In your instructions at the station, direct adults to encourage children to glue the two pieces together to create a puppet. Also emphasize the importance of children completing the work themselves. Mention the importance of a child's hands-on experience over the importance of the quality of the end product. Provide supplies for decorating the puppets, such as markers, googly eyes, buttons, and stickers. Suggest

that the children take the puppets home to perform puppet shows about their favorite stories.

Note: When the program time has reached the end, begin singing your closing song. Ask the children to put supplies away at this point during the program each week. Meet adults and children at the door and remind them of the next session as they leave.

Closing Song: "Goodbye, My Friends"
(to the tune of "Goodnight, Ladies")

> Goodbye, my friends.
> Goodbye, my friends.
> Goodbye, my friends.
> I hope to see you soon.
> *(repeat)*

LESSON PLAN: WEEK 2

ECRR practice: Singing
Readiness domain focus: Approaches to learning, social-emotional development, language development

---

Introduction

Introduce this week's skill focus area: singing. Explain that singing helps develop early literacy skills through slowing down the sounds in words and through natural rhythm, which helps children prepare for reading.

Opening Song: "Talk, Sing, Read, Write, Play"
(to the tune of "Goodnight, Ladies")

> Talk, sing, read, write, play,
> Talk, sing, read, write, play,
> Talk, sing, read, write, play,
> Talk, sing, read, write, play.
> *(repeat)*

Book/song: *Pete the Cat: I Love My White Shoes*

by Eric Litwin (HarperCollins, Reprint 2010)

Adult/child aside: "Choosing books that include songs and rhythm helps children to connect sounds and language to the printed text in the book. We are going to read a story about a cat who tells part of the story through singing. You will all be able to help sing the song as we go."

Note: Narration done by the author of the book and song can be downloaded for free at www.harpercollins.com/childrens/feature/petethecat.

Song: "Something in My Shoe"

by Raffi (Rise and Shine, Rounder 1996)

Book: *Farmyard Beat*

by Lindsey Craig; illustrated by Marc Brown (Random House Children's Books, 2011)

Note: This book contains rhythmic and rhyming text that helps tell the story. Be sure to encourage everyone to participate in clapping rhythms and guessing the animals that are described by the rhyming text.

Song/puppets: "Old MacDonald Had a Farm"

Note: Choose puppets that represent a variety of farm animals. Keep the puppets hidden in a basket or bag until you sing each one in the song. Singing the sounds made by animals helps children connect the sounds in the song to spoken language, an important step toward developing reading skills.

Book/fingerplay: Five Little Ducks

(Raffi Songs to Read) by Raffi; illustrated by Ariane Dewey and Jose Aruego (Random House Children's Books, Reprint 1992)

Note: Hold up your fingers to represent each of the five little ducks as you sing this song. Encourage children and parents to do the same, and to put their fingers down as fewer ducks return to the mother duck each time.

Interaction Stations

Note: Remind adults and children that there are instructions placed at each station and that it is important for everyone to participate in the interactive activities at each station.

1. **Mini stage:** Create a mini stage and encourage children to put on a concert for the adults by singing into echo microphones.
2. **Finger puppets:** Provide finger puppets that match a picture book such as Five Little Ducks. Encourage children and adults to practice telling the story with the finger puppets.
3. **Songs in books:** Feature a display of books with traditional children's songs and encourage adults and children to sing the songs as they read the books together.
4. **Craft—shaker eggs:** Provide plastic eggs, rice, dried beans and colorful electric tape. Instruct adults to encourage their children to scoop rice and/or beans into an egg and snap it closed. Adults should help children secure electric tape around the egg, and children should use the scissors to cut the tape. You may also provide stickers for children to decorate their shaker eggs. Rhythm instruments help children hear the natural rhythm of spoken language.

Closing Song: "Goodbye, My Friends"
(to the tune of "Goodnight, Ladies")

> Goodbye, my friends.
> Goodbye, my friends.
> Goodbye, my friends.
> I hope to see you soon.
> *(repeat)*

LESSON PLAN: WEEK 3

ECRR practice: Reading
Readiness domain focus: Approaches to learning, social-emotional development, language development

---

Introduction

Introduce this week's skill focus area: reading. Explain how all the activities that you have been doing so far have been helping to build children's skills to learn to read later. Tell adults that this week you are going to focus on specific early literacy skills.

Opening Song: "Talk, Sing, Read, Write, Play"
(to the tune of "Goodnight, Ladies")

> Talk, sing, read, write, play,
> Talk, sing, read, write, play,
> Talk, sing, read, write, play,
> Talk, sing, read, write, play.
> *(repeat)*

Song: "Jump"
by Nancy Stewart (Song of the Month, NancyMusic.com, 2010)

Adult aside: "Today we are going to focus on several specific pre-reading skills that help a child get ready for reading. The first skill is a child's awareness of printed words."

To children: "We are going to read a story in a minute with the word 'jump' in it. The word 'jump' begins with the letter 'j.' Before we read the word 'jump' in our book, we are going to spell it together in a song."

Note: Place large letters that spell the word "jump" on the magnet board or flannel board. Say each letter as you place your hand on it, and tell the children that the letters spell "jump" when they are put together. Use the letters to help the children sing the song.

Book: *Jump!*
by Scott M. Fischer (Simon & Schuster Books for Young Readers, 2010)

Song/large-motor movement: "Marching Around the Alphabet"
by Hap Palmer (from Learning Basic Skills through Music,
Volume 1, Educational Activities, 1969)

Adult/child aside: "Now we are going to play a game. I am going to place all the letters of the alphabet in a circle on the floor. Everyone is going to stand up and march around the circle when the music plays. When you hear the whistle blow, everyone needs to stop. Children, pick up the letter in front of you, and tell your adult what letter you have and what sound it makes. Try to think of some words that start with your letter. When you hear the song tell you, place the letter back on the floor and start marching again until the whistle blows again."

Note: Encourage the adults to help their children by guiding them through the process.

Book: *Bee & Bird*

by Craig Frazier (Roaring Book Press, 2011)

Note: Ask the children if they think you can read a book together that has no words printed on the page. As you read the story together, ask the children to tell you what is in each of the illustrations. When you have finished the book, point out to the children and adults that you were able to read a book without words. Wordless books help children connect to the illustrations, which helps them develop vocabulary and narrative skills.

Book: *I Read Signs*

by Tana Hoban (Greenwillow Books, Reprint 1987)

Adult aside: "Environmental print is text that children begin to recognize from the world around them before they can actually read it. Street, restaurant, and store signs as well as product logos are all examples of different types of environmental print. Recognizing this type of print is one of the first steps a child takes toward reading the printed word."

Group activity: Hold up a variety of different signs that children may see in their everyday lives, including such things as a stop sign, an exit sign, product logos, and familiar store or restaurant signs. Ask the children to tell you what they think each sign says.

Interaction Stations

Note: Remind adults and children that there are instructions placed at each station and that it is important for everyone to participate in the interactive activities at each station.

1. **Magazine picture storytelling:** Cut out several pages from a magazine and laminate them beforehand. Place them at the station with instructions for the adults and children to make up stories about what they think is happening in each of the pictures.
2. **Large Picture Books:** Place large lap-sized picture books in a station on the floor. Encourage adults and children to read them together.
3. **Silent version of "Red Light, Green Light":** Provide a printed stop sign on a wooden craft stick and a green go sign. Encourage adults and children to take turns being the person who holds up the sign and the person who moves. This encourages environmental print awareness and turn-taking skills.
4. **Craft—recipe card collage:** Provide several craft supplies (feathers, pompoms, cotton balls, googly eyes, buttons, markers, crayons, etc.). Create

small "recipe" cards that have pictures of the supplies on them. Turn the cards face down on the table. Supply construction paper and glue for each of the items to be glued onto as the child turns over the card with the picture of that item. Encourage adults to support their child's creativity by allowing them to create whatever they like with each of the items on their collage.

Closing Song: "Goodbye, My Friends"
(to the tune of "Goodnight, Ladies")

Goodbye, my friends.
Goodbye, my friends.
Goodbye, my friends.
I hope to see you soon.
(repeat)

LESSON PLAN: WEEK 4

ECRR practice: Writing
Readiness domain focus: Cognition and general knowledge, physical well-being and motor development, language development

Opening Song: "Talk, Sing, Read, Write, Play"
(to the tune of "Goodnight, Ladies")

Talk, sing, read, write, play,
Talk, sing, read, write, play,
Talk, sing, read, write, play,
Talk, sing, read, write, play.
(repeat)

Adult/child aside: "We are going to talk about writing today. Drawing is an important activity that leads to writing. We are going to explore lots of books and activities that will help your child work on skills that they need as they get ready to write."

Book: *Lines that Wiggle*
by Candace Whitman (Blue Apple Books, 2009)

Song/Fingerplay: "Write Your Name"

(to the tune of "If You're Happy and You Know It")

Note: Give the children a name tag or name plate with their names printed on them. Encourage the children to use their pointer fingers to trace their names as you sing the song.

> Write your name in the air, in the air.
> Write your name in the air in the air.
> Oh, hold it way up there, and write your name in the air,
> Write your name, in the air, in the air.

> Write your name on the floor, on the floor.
> Write your name on the floor, on the floor.
> We can't ask for anymore, than your name on the floor,
> Write your name on the floor, on the floor.

> Write your name in your lap, in your lap.
> Write your name in your lap, in your lap.
> We'll give a little clap, as you write it in your lap,
> Write your name in your lap, in your lap.

Note: Collect name tags or ask children to give them to their adults to take home.

Book: *Chalk*

by Bill Thomson (Two Lions, 2010)

Chant/activity: "What If Chalk Could Talk?"

Note: Give out small chalkboards or paper to each adult, along with something to use as an eraser. As you hand out the supplies, explain to the adults that they will write (or draw, if more appropriate for your group) and the children will tell their adults what they think they have written/drawn (numbers, letters, pictures). Repeat this several times. If you give children the opportunity to do the drawing/writing, change your instructions so that the children draw and then they tell their adults about what they drew. Doing it this way, the children will feel more successful than if the adults have to guess what the children drew. Recite the poem below as participants write or draw.

Adults Drawing/Writing

> What if chalk could talk?
> What would it say?
> I would like to write (*or* draw) today.

I will write (*or* draw),
Then you tell me,
What it is you think you see.

(Children tell their adults about the letter or drawing that they observe.)

CHILDREN DRAWING/WRITING

What if chalk could talk?
What would it say?
I would like to write (*or* draw) today.
I will write (*or* draw),
Then tell you,
About the thing I wrote (*or* drew) for you.

(Children tell you about the letter or drawing that they drew for you.)

Note: Collect the supplies from the group before moving to the next book.

Book: *A Day with No Crayons*
by Elizabeth Rusch; illustrated by Chad Cameron (Cooper Square Publishing, 2007)

Interaction Stations: Drawing without Crayons

Note: Remind adults and children that there are instructions placed at each station and that it is important for everyone to participate in the interactive activities at each station.

Place different writing/drawing utensils at each station. Encourage children to move from station to station with their adults to create one picture using the items at each of the stations. Remind the children that they are drawing something without crayons. Remind the adults that drawing with different types of tools helps children to develop the skills needed for writing. The list below is a suggestion—you can add other tools that you might have that would also be appropriate.

1. **Chalk Table**
2. **Markers Table**
3. **Colored-Pencil Table**
4. **Dot Marker/Bingo Marker Table**

Note: You may want to add three-dimensional objects, as well, such as buttons, feathers, and pom-poms. Use anything other than crayons to encourage children to create a picture.

Closing Song: "Goodbye, My Friends"

(to the tune of "Goodnight, Ladies")

> Goodbye, my friends.
> Goodbye, my friends.
> Goodbye, my friends.
> I hope to see you soon.
> *(repeat)*

LESSON PLAN: WEEK 5

ECRR practice: Playing
Readiness domain focus: Approaches to learning, cognition and general knowledge, social-emotional development, language development

Opening Song: "Talk, Sing, Read, Write, Play"

(to the tune of "Goodnight, Ladies")

> Talk, sing, read, write, play,
> Talk, sing, read, write, play,
> Talk, sing, read, write, play,
> Talk, sing, read, write, play.
> *(repeat)*

Adult aside: "Play is a child's work. Children learn how to get along with others and take turns through play. They also learn about the world around them through play. We are going to do some play-based activities today that will provide the opportunity for your child to work on school readiness and literacy skills while they play with each other and with you."

Book: *Llama Llama Time to Share*

by Anna Dewdney (Viking Juvenile, 2012)

Song/Fingerplay: "I Like to Play with Friends"

(to the tune of "Here We Go 'Round the Mulberry Bush")

> I like to play with friends,
> I like to play with friends,
> Hi, ho, and here we go,
> I like to play with friends.

I like to share with friends,
I like to share with friends,
Hi, ho, and here we go,
I like to share with friends.

I like to laugh with friends,
I like to laugh with friends,
Hi, ho, and here we go,
I like to laugh with friends.

I like to sit with friends,
I like to sit with friends,
Hi, ho, and here we go,
I like to sit with friends.

Note: Use different gestures or sign language for each action listed in the song. You can find simple sign language resources at the website Baby Sign Language (www.babysignlanguage.com).

Book: *The Story of Fish & Snail*
by Deborah Freedman (Viking Juvenile, 2013)

Song/motor movement: "The Goldfish"
by Laurie Berkner (Victor Vito, Two Tomatoes, 2001)

Note: Talk about how this song uses imagination to make goldfish do things that they cannot really do. Cut out die-cut fish to give to the children, and encourage them to swim/dance with their fish.

Book: *Not a Box*
by Antoinette Portis (HarperCollins, 2006)

Note: Talk to the children about how the character uses his imagination to turn a box into many different things. Talk about what "pretend" is, and how the children and adults will get to pretend at one of the interaction stations this week.

Interaction Stations

Note: Remind adults and children that there are instructions placed at each station and that it is important for everyone to participate in the interactive activities at each station.

Adult/child aside: "We are going to use our imagination to pretend just like the rabbit in the story. We have many stations set up for everyone to play together. You may start at any station you would like and then we will rotate. I will give everyone a countdown of how much time remains as you play. When you hear me begin the goodbye song, everyone needs to put the materials back in their bins and get ready to go."

1. **Pizza parlor:** Request a couple of unused pizza boxes from a local pizza restaurant for use at this station. Prepare items before your program by cutting a circular crust from light brown felt, pepperoni circles and sauce from red felt, and cheese from yellow yarn. Set out all the items for children to make pizzas. Create menus with clip-art pictures that represent each of the toppings and print the price for each. Make order pads out of small notebooks. Encourage adults and children to take turns being the customers, servers, and chefs.

2. **Cooperative play:** Supply blown-up balloons at this station for children and adults to keep up in the air. Encourage each adult-and-child pair to softly hit the balloon back and forth while saying the entire alphabet. Adults and children can take turns saying a letter each time it is their turn to hit the balloon.

3. **Post office:** Provide envelopes, paper, pencils, junk mail, and stickers for adults and children to create their own pieces of mail. Before the program, create a mailbox from a large appliance box with a slit cut for the drop box. Encourage adults and children to add the mail to the drop box.

4. **Craft—play dough:** Provide play dough to play with during the program or to take home. Make homemade play dough beforehand and place a ball for each child in a sealed baggie. Provide cookie cutters, rolling pins, and other tools to use with the play dough at the table. Playing with play dough is a great sensory-based activity that also helps children strengthen the hand muscles needed for writing.

Closing Song: "Goodbye, My Friends"
(to the tune of "Goodnight, Ladies")

Goodbye, my friends.
Goodbye, my friends.
Goodbye, my friends.
I hope to see you soon.
(repeat)

LESSON PLAN: WEEK 6

ECRR practice: Self-help and motor skills
Readiness domain focus: Approaches to learning, physical well-being and motor development, social-emotional development

Introduction

Remind adults and children that this is the last session of the program. Present certificates at the end of the session. You may want to consider giving each child a picture book about kindergarten if it is feasible for your library.

You may want to invite kindergarten teachers to attend this session. If possible, teachers can participate in reading one of the books or can lead a song during this session.

Opening Song: "Talk, Sing, Read, Write, Play"

(to the tune of "Goodnight, Ladies")

> Talk, sing, read, write, play,
> Talk, sing, read, write, play,
> Talk, sing, read, write, play,
> Talk, sing, read, write, play.
> *(repeat)*

Adult/child aside: "This week we will do activities together that work on self-help and movement skills, as well as health and social development."

Book: *All By Myself*

by Aliki (HarperCollins, 2003)

Chant/fingerplay: "All By Myself"

Note: Encourage adults and children to chant the "all by myself" lines, and to act out the motions with you for each activity in the chant.

> What can I do (all by myself)?
> Here's what I can do (all by myself) . . .
> I can wash my hands (all by myself).
> I can comb my hair (all by myself).
> I can put on my shoes (all by myself).
> What can you do (all by yourself)?

(continued)

Point to one of the children and ask them to act out and say something that they can do all by themselves. Continue this until all children have had a turn. End with the following lines:

> I can sit right down (all by myself),
> And fold my hands (all by myself).

Book: *Look Out Kindergarten, Here I Come!*
by Nancy Carlson (Puffin, Reprint 2001)

Fingerplay: "This Is the Way My Scissors Cut"

Note: Demonstrate the way children cut with scissors by holding your first two fingers together, and place your thumb on top, just as you would hold scissors. Ask the adults to help their children hold their fingers the same way. Show children how the thumb stays on top, and demonstrate how to open and close your fingers as you would with scissors. Say the following chant through the first time while opening and closing fingers, and then encourage the children and adults to do it with you the second time.

> Open, shut,
> Open shut,
> This is the way my scissors cut.
> Open, shut,
> Open, shut,
> This is the way I cut, cut, cut.

Book: *My Many Colored Days*
by Dr. Seuss; Illustrated by Steve Johnson and Lou Fancher
(Knopf Books for Young Readers, 1996)

Song: A Variation on "If You're Happy and You Know It"

> If you're happy and you know it, clap your hands.
> If you're happy and you know it, clap your hands.
> If you're happy and you know it, and you really want to show it,
> If you're happy and you know it, clap your hands.
>
> If you're sad and you know it, sniff and pout . . .
>
> If you're silly and you know it, giggle and jiggle . . .

If you're angry and you know it, cross your arms . . .

If you're scared and you know it, give a shiver . . .

If you're sleepy and you know it, give a yawn . . .

If you're happy and you know it, . . .

Interaction Stations

1. **Cutting practice:** Provide safety scissors and different items for children to practice cutting, such as drinking straws, play dough, paper strips, and magazines. Encourage adults to remind children to place their thumb in the top hole of the scissors and their first two fingers in the bottom. Adults can help guide their child's cutting by verbal prompts, such as "open, shut, open, shut,"

2. **Game—"See What I Can Do All By Myself":** Print out different physical "challenges" onto cardstock and cut them into small cards. Place the cards face down on a table at the station. Ask adults to turn over the cards one at the time and read the challenges to their child. Challenges should not be overly difficult, and adults should encourage their children to try each challenge. Challenges can include movements such as taking off shoes, jumping three times, counting, and saying the alphabet.

3. **Button sorting:** Provide different-colored buttons and cups for children to sort them into. Sorting is an important skill that helps children develop math and literacy skills, while picking up buttons develops the hand strength needed for developing writing skills.

4. **Craft—"Paint the Way You Feel":** Supply construction paper and water colors. Play different types of music and encourage children to paint how the music makes them feel.

Closing Song: "Goodbye, My Friends"
(to the tune of "Goodnight, Ladies")

Goodbye, my friends.
Goodbye, my friends.
Goodbye, my friends.
I hope to see you soon.
(repeat)

FIGURE 6.1
Red Apple

FIGURE 6.2
Orange Carrot

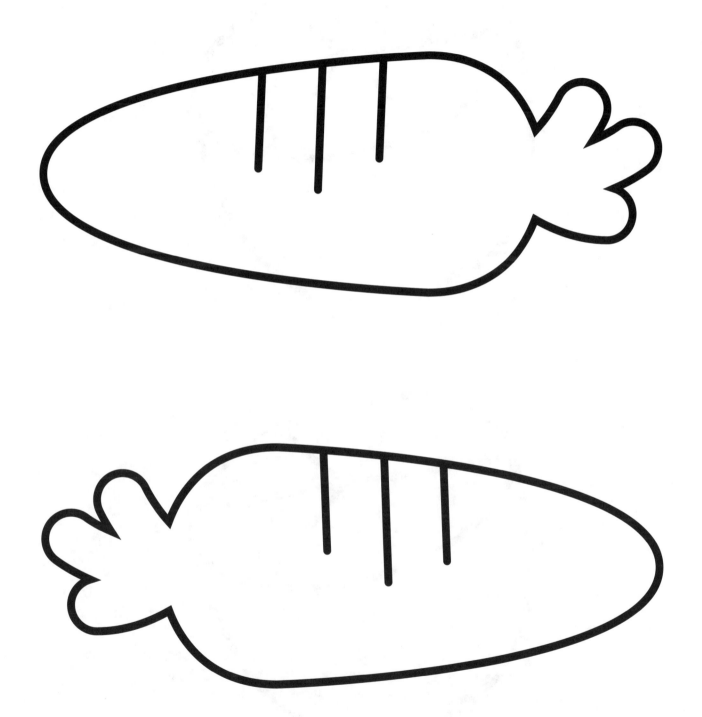

FIGURE 6.3
Yellow Lemon

FIGURE 6.4
Green Frog

FIGURE 6.5
Blue and Indigo Sky

FIGURE 6.6
Puppet

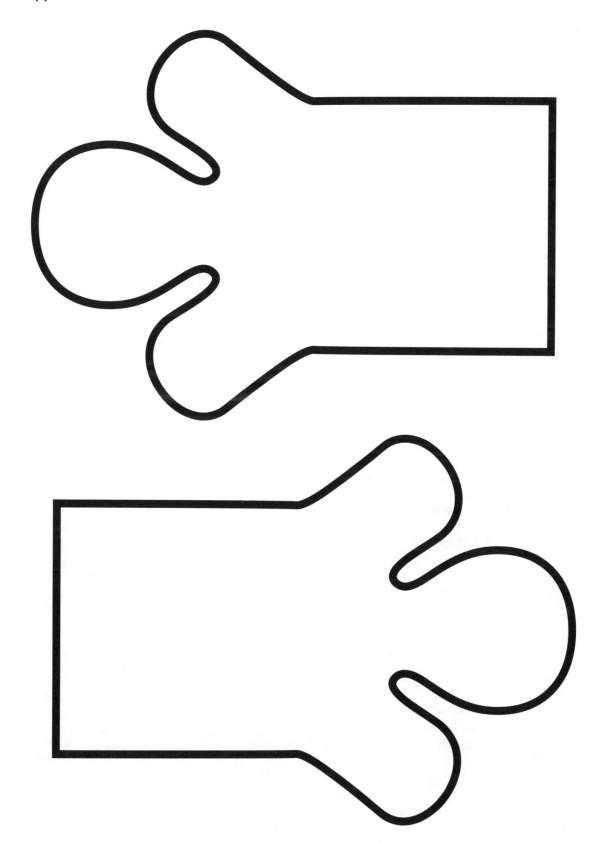

CHAPTER 7

HOW THE
Readiness Calendar
WAS DEVELOPED

AND HOW TO DEVELOP YOUR OWN

THE CALENDAR INCLUDED IN THIS BOOK IS BASED ON THE original calendar created for the school readiness program at Paul Sawyier Public Library in Frankfort, Kentucky. The calendar is distributed during the adult/child sessions of our Countdown to Kindergarten program, which is offered the semester before a child enters kindergarten. The calendar is distributed during the first session of the program, and parents are encouraged to complete the calendar activities at home during the months before their children begin kindergarten. Prior to developing the program and this calendar, I met with kindergarten teachers in the community to determine the readiness skills that were important to include. I gathered information from the schools regarding the required records for kindergarten registration, and this information is included on the back of the original calendar. This information can be added easily to the back cover of your own calendars after you meet with your community schools, as well. (See chapter four for more in-depth information on building collaborative relationships with teachers.)

What Is Included on the Readiness Calendar

The calendar included at the end of this chapter is a six-month calendar that corresponds with the content of the lesson plans in chapter six. The calendar is intended to be reproduced and distributed to the parents/caregivers who attend your school readiness program with their child. The suggested activities included on the calendar are meant for parents to do at home with children as they prepare for the transition to kindergarten. The first five months of the calendar focus on each of the five early literacy practices from Every Child Ready to Read 2: talking, singing, reading, writing, and playing.[1] The sixth month of the calendar focuses on self-help and motor skills—two areas identified by kindergarten teachers as the most important for successfully transitioning into kindergarten.

Each month of the calendar includes facts about the skill focus area addressed that month. Book lists and at-home activities are included to help parents focus on specific skills. The activities are simple things that parents/caregivers should be able to do with their children as part of their everyday routine. It is important for children to be able to connect what they learn to their everyday lives. In this way, new knowledge becomes more concrete, and this helps children generalize new knowledge across environments and situations—an important milestone of early childhood development.

How to Use the Calendar Included in this Book

Monthly headers and dates are not included on the calendar pages so that you may distribute them during any month of the year to coincide with your own program. At-home activities are highlighted on the calendar, and notes for parents/caregivers appear at the bottom of each calendar page. These notes explain the importance of the month's early literacy practice and also list the month's readiness domain.

This calendar is available in black and white at the end of this chapter, or in color as a downloadable PDF at alaeditions.org/webextras. It is best to photocopy the calendar double-sided in landscape setting. This should enable you to simply flip up the pages of the calendar to view the next month. You should be able to view it on the bottom of the page with the skill information on the top page. The calen-

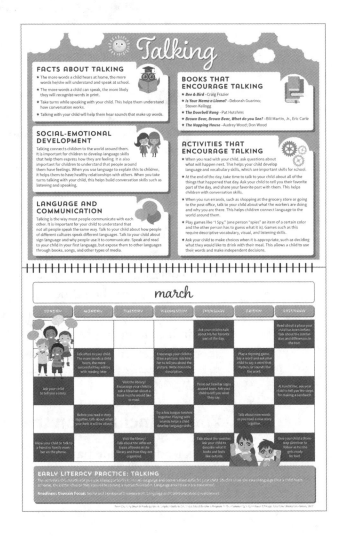

dar can be stapled together, or, if you have access to a comb-binding machine, it works well as a spiral-bound calendar. Covers can be copied onto cardstock and laminated in order to make the calendar sturdier.

How to Use the Web-Extra Customizable Calendar

A *fully customizable* calendar is also offered as a downloadable Microsoft Word file at alaeditions.org/webextras. Specific skills that correspond with your calendar activities—and are identified as needs within your own community—can be inserted at the bottom of each month. In order to determine your community's needs, ask for information from kindergarten teachers within your own community. It is also important that you become familiar with your state's definition of school readiness, and that you know about your community's kindergarten entrance screening results. If your state has a governor's office of early childhood, you can find this information through their office, or you can also contact one of the public school preschool or Head Start offices in your state. The calendar will be most useful to your program participants if you take the time to customize the information in these ways. Your program will have the biggest impact on your entire community if you also make these connections throughout your entire program.

Adding Specific School and Community Information to Your Calendar

As noted, specific information from your own community's schools can be added to the inside cover of your calendar, or as an additional page inserted within your calendar. Contact information for each school can be added, as well as additional information about getting a library card or signing up for other programs at your library. You might also choose to add information about other early childhood organizations from your community and how families might go about contacting them. If you need additional funding for printing calendars, consider seeking sponsors to highlight within your calendar. This not only could help you fund the publication of your calendars, but could also provide important information for families to connect to other early childhood services within the community. The back cover of your calendar could also be reserved for sponsor logos or ads.

Other Options

If your library's funding does not allow you to print and distribute the entire readiness calendar, you may choose to reproduce only the actual calendar month pages. You may simply use the skill and practice pages as a script to verbally share or post information about the importance of these skills. The calendar pages provide activities that connect to these skills, so it is vital that the information is communicated; but if funding limits your ability to reproduce the entire calendar, the home-activity portion of the calendar will at least provide skill practice for families at home.

Another option is to distribute a one-month calendar, like the example on page 73, if you offer a onetime program. The one-month calendar should include activities that are connected to all five early literacy practices and domains of readiness. In this way, participants will still receive a resource that will help them understand what types of activities they should do at home to help prepare their children for school.

How to Develop Your Own Calendar

Another option might be to build a longer calendar and make it available online. This is especially useful for libraries who cannot fund printing a longer calendar. You can add the calendar to your library's website, create a free blog, or simply develop a Google calendar and send the link to parents/caregivers. Information from early childhood service organizations can be added to an online calendar, along with pertinent information from community schools and kindergarten teachers. Upcoming kindergarten registration and other important dates can be added easily to an online calendar. You may even choose to produce an online calendar as an additional supplement to your printed calendar to cover a longer period of time.

If you opt to develop your own printable calendar, you can create each month with a standard program, such as Microsoft Office. Simply add activities that are easy to do at home during a typical family's schedule. As with the one-month calendar, connect activity suggestions to each of the five Every Child Ready to Read best practices and each of your state's readiness domain indicators of readiness. It is important to match the skill focus to the calendar activities for the month, as well to add book suggestions that foster those skills—aligning your program lesson plans with the calendar is essential. A good rule of thumb is to provide a five- or six-month calendar. This will allow you to link each month to one of the five best practices of Every Child Ready to Read. Each week of your program should correspond with the focus area of one of the months. In the event that you choose to create a six-week program and calendar, the final week/calendar month can focus on skills that your community kindergarten teachers identify as important, such as fine motor and self-help skills.

Promotional Materials

After you have finished your calendars and planned your programs, promote it throughout the early childhood community. Be sure to announce the program to members of your community early childhood council, local early care facilities, preschool classrooms, and kindergarten classrooms. Also post promotional materials in places that families visit, such as pediatricians' offices, laundromats, community centers, and on community bulletin boards.

In order to promote your school readiness program, create a one-month version of the readiness calendar. This calendar should not be an exact reproduction of any of the months in your six-month readiness calendar, but a separate promotional calendar that incorporates readiness skills and literacy practices into one month (see figure 7.1). A customizable one-month calendar is available as a Microsoft Word file at alaeditions.org/webextras. This calendar can be used to

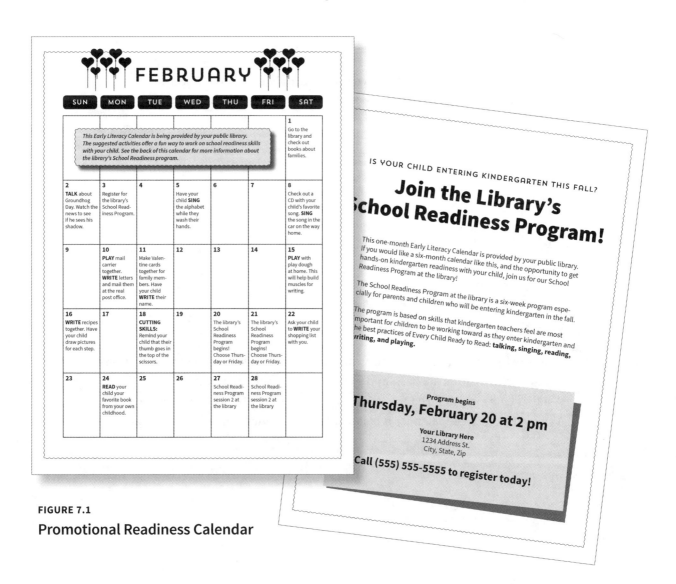

FIGURE 7.1
Promotional Readiness Calendar

send home with current patrons or to share with area preschools and early care facilities. When it is time for kindergarten registration, this promotional calendar can also be given to schools in order to reach parents who are registering their children for kindergarten.

On the other side of the calendar, text can also be added with more specific information about program dates and times, and registration procedures.

The full six-month readiness calendar follows this chapter. It should be copied front and back in order to create a calendar that parents can hang up at home. Please feel free to reproduce this calendar by copying it directly for your readiness programs; however, copyright information should not be removed from the bottom of each page. A color version is also available to download from alaeditions.org/webextras.

Note

1. Elaine Meyers and Harriet Henderson, "Overview of Every Child Ready to Read @ your library, 1st Edition," Every Child Ready to Read @ your library, accessed January 18, 2015, www.everychildreadytoread.org/project-history%09/overview-every-child-ready-read-your-library%C2%AE-1st-edition.

The Readiness Calendar

Copy the following 13 pages (or download and print the color PDF at alaeditions.org/webextras) front to back and head to toe. Staple or bind at the top edge. Write in your personalized months, or copy and paste the months from page 88. A fully customizable calendar is also available as a Microsoft Word file.

COUNTING DOWN *to* Kindergarten

Talking

BOOKS THAT ENCOURAGE TALKING

* *Bee & Bird* –Craig Frazier
* *Is Your Mama a Llama?* –Deborah Guarino; Steven Kellogg
* *The Doorbell Rang* –Pat Hutchins
* *Brown Bear, Brown Bear, What do you See?* – Bill Martin, Jr., Eric Carle
* *The Napping House* –Audrey Wood; Don Wood

ACTIVITIES THAT ENCOURAGE TALKING

* When you read with your child, ask questions about what will happen next. This helps your child develop language and vocabulary skills, which are important skills for school.

* At the end of the day, take time to talk to your child about all of the things that happened that day. Ask your child to tell you their favorite part of the day, and share your favorite part with them. This helps children with conversation skills.

* When you run errands, such as shopping at the grocery store or going to the post office, talk to your child about what the workers are doing and why you are there. This helps children connect language to the world around them.

* Play games like "I Spy," (one person "spies" an item of a certain color and the other person has to guess what it is). Games such as this require descriptive vocabulary, visual, and listening skills.

* Ask your child to make choices when it is appropriate, such as deciding what they would like to drink with their meal. This allows a child to use their words and make independent decisions.

FACTS ABOUT TALKING

* The more words a child hears at home, the more words he/she will understand and speak at school.

* The more words a child can speak, the more likely they will recognize words in print.

* Take turns while speaking with your child. This helps them understand how conversation works.

* Talking with your child will help them hear sounds that make up words.

SOCIAL-EMOTIONAL DEVELOPMENT

Talking connects children to the world around them. It is important for children to develop language skills that help them express how they are feeling. It is also important for children to understand that people around them have feelings. When you use language to explain this to children, it helps them to have healthy relationships with others. When you take turns talking with your child, this helps build conversation skills such as listening and speaking.

LANGUAGE AND COMMUNICATION

Talking is the way most people communicate with each other. It is important for your child to understand that not all people speak the same way. Talk to your child about how people of different cultures speak different languages. Talk to your child about sign language and why people use it to communicate. Speak and read to your child in your first language, but expose them to other languages through books, songs, and other types of media.

EARLY LITERACY PRACTICE: TALKING

SUNDAY	MONDAY	TUESDAY	WEDNESDAY	THURSDAY	FRIDAY	SATURDAY
	Talk often to your child. The more words a child hears, the more successful they will be with reading later.		Encourage your child to draw a picture. Ask him/her to tell you about the picture. Write down the description.	Ask your child to talk about his/her favorite part of the day.	Play a rhyming game. Say a word and ask your child to say a word that rhymes, or sounds like the word.	Read about a place your child has been before. Talk about the similarities and differences in the text.
Ask your child to tell you a story.		Visit the library! Encourage your child to ask a librarian about a book he/she would like to read.				
	Before you read a story together, talk about what you think it will be about.		Try a few tongue twisters together. Playing with sounds helps a child develop language skills.	Point out familiar signs around town. Ask your child to tell you what they say.	Talk about new words as you read a new story together.	At lunchtime, ask your child to tell you the steps for making a sandwich.
Allow your child to talk to a friend or family member on the phone.		Visit the library! Talk about the different types of books in the library and how they are organized.		Talk about the weather. Ask your child to describe what it looks and feels like outside.		Give your child a three-step direction to follow as he/she gets ready for bed.

The activities this month will give you the opportunity to model language and conversation skills for your child. Studies show the more language that a child hears at home, the better chance they have of becoming a successful reader. Language and literacy are connected.

Readiness Domain Focus: Social and Emotional Development, Language and Communication Development

From *Counting Down to Kindergarten: A Complete Guide to Creating a School Readiness Program for Your Community*, R. Lynn Baker (Chicago: American Library Association, 2015).

Singing

FACTS ABOUT SINGING

* Singing is important because it slows language down. This helps children hear individual sounds in words.

* Singing and music stimulates all different parts of the brain, which helps with reading and learning.

* Music encourages movement with young children that helps develop coordination and muscle strength.

SOCIAL-EMOTIONAL DEVELOPMENT

Music and movement activities such as singing and dancing foster self-confidence and self-awareness. Singing in a group helps a child connect with peers. Music-based activities help children to explore new ideas and new words. Singing with others encourages children to share the "spotlight." This helps children better understand the idea of sharing and turn-taking.

LANGUAGE AND COMMUNICATION

Children can hear the sounds that make up individual words through singing. Children also have the opportunity to learn new words through singing new songs. Songs often rhyme, which helps introduce this literacy concept. The rhythm of the music helps prepare children to hear the rhythm of reading. Children can learn new concepts through songs that introduce math, science, history, different cultures, different languages, sequencing . . . the list goes on and on.

BOOKS THAT ENCOURAGE SINGING

* *Dancing Feet* – Lindsey Craig; Marc Brown
* *Pete the Cat: I Love My White Shoes* – James Dean; Eric Litwin
* *De Colores: Bright with Colors* – David Diaz
* *Chicka, Chicka Boom Boom* –Bill Martin, Jr.; John Archambault; Lois Ehlert
* *Raffi Songs to Read* series –Raffi

MUSIC THAT ENCOURAGES SINGING

* *Whaddaya Think of That* – Laurie Berkner
* *Smile at Your Neighbor* – Eric Litwin
* *The Singable Songs Collection* – Raffi
* *Music Time with SteveSongs* – SteveSongs

ACTIVITIES THAT ENCOURAGE SINGING

* Check out CDs or downloadable music from the library. What you think is important, your child will see as important. If you model a love of music and reading, your child is more likely to do the same.

* Learn songs with your child. Allow your child to listen to the music in the car or at home.

* Make up silly songs together. This helps your child play with the sounds in language.

* Clap out the syllables in words with your child. This will help your child understand how words are broken up into parts.

* Play music during quiet times at home. The rhythm of music stimulates the brain.

SUNDAY	MONDAY	TUESDAY	WEDNESDAY	THURSDAY	FRIDAY	SATURDAY
Sing familiar songs that play with sounds, such as "I Like to Eat Apples and Bananas."		Visit the library! Check out some music to play at home or in the car with your child.		Encourage your child to make up their own songs.		Sing the day's schedule to the tune of Twinkle, Twinkle, Little Star.
	Sing the alphabet song together, and then encourage your child to sing it alone.		Clap out the syllables as you sing a sing together.		Purchase an inexpensive echo microphone. Encourage your child to put on a concert for you.	
Encourage your child to make up his/her own words to a familiar tune.		Visit the library! Check out a book that is a song you can sing together.		Make a drum together using an oatmeal container.		Clap a rhythm and encourage your child to repeat what he/she hears.
	Sing a song with letters, such as BINGO.		Sing a song that tells a story, such as Mary had a Little Lamb.		Sing songs together in the car.	
Sing a song that encourages your child to echo or repeat you.		Ask your child to pick out a song to sing together each morning.				

EARLY LITERACY PRACTICE: SINGING

The activities this month will help you foster language skills through slowing down the sounds in language. Singing and music also helps children to understand rhythm, which helps with developing skills necessary for reading.

Readiness Domain Focus: Approaches to Learning; Language and Communication; Social and Emotional Development

From *Counting Down to Kindergarten: A Complete Guide to Creating a School Readiness Program for Your Community*, R. Lynn Baker (Chicago: American Library Association, 2015).

Reading

FACTS ABOUT READING

* Reading together is important! You are your child's first and best teacher. If you show your child that reading is important, they will think it is important, too.

* Reading skills begin at birth . . . language and literacy go hand in hand.

* When children look at picture books before they can read the words on the page, they are working on important skills that will lead to reading.

* Reading the same book over and over helps children connect spoken words to the text on the page.

APPROACHES TO LEARNING

A child's attitude about learning—especially reading—impacts how successful he/she will be. When children are taught that reading is fun, they are much more likely to want to learn, and more likely to continue reading as they become older. How children perceive reading has a big impact on all areas of learning. It is important to make learning fun, and for your child to see you enjoying reading and learning, as well.

LANGUAGE AND COMMUNICATION

Reading together fosters language skills, and introduces new ideas and concepts to your child. Encouraging your child to participate in reading through asking questions helps children to develop their own story-telling and narrative skills. Interactive reading also helps a child learn the sequence of events and helps them to see the connection between the words and the pictures on the page. When adults read to children, this provides practice with listening skills and making sense of the information they hear.

BOOKS THAT ENCOURAGE READING

* *The Very Hungry Caterpillar* –Eric Carle

* *Pete the Cat and His Four Groovy Buttons* –James Dean; Eric Litwin

* *Bark, George* – Jules Feiffer

* *If You Give a Mouse a Cookie* –Laura Numeroff; Felicia Bond

* *The Lion and the Mouse* –Jerry Pinkney

ACTIVITIES THAT ENCOURAGE READING

* Read together 20 minutes per day. Research shows that this simple practice has a big impact on a child's success as a reader later.

* Create a cozy space for your child to read. Place books on a shelf that is easy for them to reach. Have a "reading time" every day when you read a book and your child reads a book alone. Modeling this type of reading will help develop your child's reading skills later.

* Read signs when you are out with your child. Children will recognize familiar print—this is a child's first step toward reading.

* Read wordless books together. Ask your child to read the story to you through the actions in the pictures. This offers your child the opportunity to be the narrator and helps to develop language, communication, and literacy skills.

* Choose books to read to your child that you find enjoyable. If you enjoy a book, chances are your child will, too. When reading is fun, it has a much more positive impact on a child!

SUNDAY	MONDAY	TUESDAY	WEDNESDAY	THURSDAY	FRIDAY	SATURDAY
Create a cozy area with books for your child to sit and read with you.		Visit the library! Check out a few rhyming books to read together.		Let your child see you reading. Talk about why you enjoy reading.		When you read to your child, ask questions about what might happen in the story.
	Re-read books together. Young children learn best through repetition.		Show your child how to hold a book and turn the pages.		Read your favorite book from childhood. Share memories from your childhood.	
Read a nonfiction book about an animal. Talk about the animal's habitat.		Visit the library! Check out a book about the library.		Read a wordless book. Encourage your child to tell you what is happening in the pictures.		Make a book with paper. Encourage your child to draw pictures to tell the story.
	Go on a letter scavenger hunt. Encourage your child to find every letter of the alphabet.		Talk with your child about the author and illustrator of the book you read together.		Choose a book you enjoy reading—when you have fun, your child learns to love reading, too.	
Point to words as you read them. This helps your child connect your language to the words on the page.		Visit the library! Check out books about things that your child is interested in.				

EARLY LITERACY PRACTICE: READING

The activities this month will help you prepare your child for becoming a successful reader. In order for children to develop reading skills, it is important for them to be read to. Taking 20 minutes per day to read together helps children understand that text on a page has meaning; develop a love for reading; recognize letters; develop listening and language skills; and helps them learn new words.

Readiness Domain Focus: Approaches to Learning; Language and Communication; Cognitive/General Knowledge

From Counting Down to Kindergarten: A Complete Guide to Creating a School Readiness Program for Your Community, R. Lynn Baker (Chicago: American Library Association, 2015).

Writing

BOOKS THAT ENCOURAGE WRITING

* *Draw Me a Star* –Eric Carle
* *Rocket Writes a Story* –Tad Hills
* *Harold and the Purple Crayon* –Crockett Johnson
* *Library Mouse (series)* –Daniel Kirk
* *More Bears!* –Kenn Nesbitt; Troy Cummings

ACTIVITIES THAT ENCOURAGE WRITING

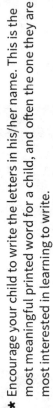
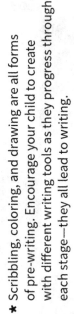

* Scribbling, coloring, and drawing are all forms of pre-writing. Encourage your child to create with different writing tools as they progress through each stage—they all lead to writing.

* Encourage your child to write the letters in his/her name. This is the most meaningful printed word for a child, and often the one they are most interested in learning to write.

* Write the alphabet on lined paper with a yellow highlighter. Encourage your child to trace letters with a pencil.

* Provide regular size pencils for children to learn with. Using fatter pencils for children to learn with actually makes it more difficult for children to learn to write with regular size tools when it is required in school. In order for your child to develop the correct pencil grip, it is important for them to have practice with the tools they will be using in school.

* Allow your child to help with the grocery list by drawing pictures of a few items and/or checking items off the list as you purchase them.

* Write letters, cards, and notes to family members and encourage your child to sign their name to cards that you give to loved ones.

FACTS ABOUT WRITING

* When a young child scribbles, it is his/her first step toward writing.

* Drawing and coloring are important activities for a child to practice in order to learn proper gripping and control of writing tools.

* Children need to practice with a variety of writing tools, including standard-size pencils, pens, crayons, markers, paintbrushes, chalk. By using different tools, children learn that each tool feels different, but accomplishes the same thing. Drawing helps children understand the meaning behind pictures.

PHYSICAL WELL-BEING / MOTOR DEVELOPMENT

Learning how to hold a pencil, crayon, marker, or pen is a fine motor skill that children learn over time. Other fine motor skills include cutting with scissors, buttoning, zipping, snapping, and tying shoes. It is important to provide opportunities for your child to strengthen hand muscles needed for these skills before they enter school.

LANGUAGE AND COMMUNICATION

Writing and drawing are important methods of communication. When your child first begins expressing ideas through drawing, it is important to ask them to tell you about what they have drawn. This gives the child the opportunity to verbally connect the ideas that they expressed on paper. To connect drawing and verbal language to written language, write down what your child tells you about their picture. This allows your child to see the connection between each type of communication, and also models writing skills for them to follow.

SUNDAY	MONDAY	TUESDAY	WEDNESDAY	THURSDAY	FRIDAY	SATURDAY
	Ask your child to help you make a grocery list by drawing pictures of some of the items.			Make many different types of writing tools available for your child to use for drawing and writing.		Write letters on writing paper with a highlighter. Encourage your child to trace over the letters with a pencil.
Allow your child to play in shaving cream on a table. Encourage them to write their name in the cream.		Visit the library! Look up books together using the catalog. Write down the call numbers together.	Play restaurant. Encourage your child to take your order and write it down, or draw it.		Write a letter together with your child and mail it to a family member.	
	Use play dough together in order for your child to strengthen hand muscles for writing.			Ask your child to draw/write a recipe card for making a sandwich.		Help your child work on making shapes with a pencil by doing connect the dot puzzles together.
Supply washable paint and brushes. Ask your child to paint a picture of you.		Visit the library! Look for books about writing and drawing.	Have a small wipe-off board and markers available for your child to practice with.	Help your child practice writing letters with their finger in the air.	Ask your child to draw different shapes with different writing tools.	

EARLY LITERACY PRACTICE: WRITING

The activities this month will help your child develop hand strength and hand-eye coordination—skills needed for writing. The activities will also promote your child's awareness of the connection between written words and language.

Readiness Domain Focus: Cognitive/General Knowledge; Language and Communication; Health and Physical Well-Being

From Counting Down to Kindergarten: A Complete Guide to Creating a School Readiness Program for Your Community, R. Lynn Baker (Chicago: American Library Association, 2015).

Playing

FACTS ABOUT PLAYING

Playing is a child's work. It is through play and exploration that a child learns most about the world around them. It is important for children to have the opportunity to play with peers and adults, as well as to play independently. Play should offer a child the opportunity to engage their senses through imaginative play: to interact with people, places, and things in their everyday world; and should incorporate print as much as possible.

SOCIAL-EMOTIONAL DEVELOPMENT

Playing with peers is important for a child's social development—one of the most important areas of readiness identified by kindergarten teachers. Play enables a child to try out new ideas and apply knowledge through using their imagination. Play also promotes getting to know others in a way that feels safe and familiar. Play helps build self esteem and confidence.

COGNITION/GENERAL KNOWLEDGE

Play helps children learn about the world around them. Play can be connected to the people and places that are a part of a child's daily living. Play that involves imagination, also called dramatic play, allows a child to learn through being actively engaged in familiar situations, such as playing house, setting up a pretend restaurant, or playing grocery store. It is important to introduce print into a child's play as much as possible, as well as to provide realistic materials—such as receipts, menus, pretend money, etc. This helps children connect play to the real world.

BOOKS THAT ENCOURAGE PLAYING

* *Five Little Monkeys Jumping on the Bed* –Eileen Christlelow

* *Let's Do Nothing!* –Tony Fucile

* *A Mouse Told His Mother* –Bethany Roberts; Maryjane Begin-Callanan

* *My Friend Rabbit* –Eric Rohmann

* *Is Everyone Ready for Fun?* –Jan Thomas

ACTIVITIES THAT ENCOURAGE PLAYING

* Provide realistic materials for children to play with, such as empty cardboard food containers for playing grocery store, or an old cell phone for playing office. Using realistic items will help children learn to interact with their world.

* Set up a pretend grocery store. Take turns playing the part of the customer and the cashier. Use stickers or pieces of paper taped to the items as price tags. Encourage your child to write the prices on the stickers. When paying for the items you purchase, use pretend money and help your child count it out. Write out pretend receipts and encourage your child to sign their name to receipts for pretend credit cards.

* Set up a post office station. Provide envelopes and paper for your child to write letters and mail them in a pretend mailbox. Use junk mail for post office play.

* Play school. Encourage your child to play the role of the teacher. This will help erase fears about starting school, while also providing an opportunity for learning.

EARLY LITERACY PRACTICE: PLAYING

SUNDAY	MONDAY	TUESDAY	WEDNESDAY	THURSDAY	FRIDAY	SATURDAY
						Allow your child to experiment with water, measuring cups, and bowls.
Act out your child's favorite book together.	Create a sensory tub with sand, beans, water, or rice. Encourage your child to scoop and pour.	Make puppets together with paper bags. Encourage your child to put on a puppet show for you.	Visit the library! Play educational games with your child on a computer.		Build a town together using blocks. Add trucks and cars and build a road.	
				Play a simple board game. This helps children learn to follow directions and take turns.		Set up a play date with another child. This helps your child develop social and turn-taking skills.
	Play "school" with your child. Take turns being the teacher.		Visit the library! Look for CDs with interactive songs and games.		Play grocery store. Encourage your child to write price tags and count money as you "buy" groceries.	
Pretend to cook with your child using pots, pans, and utensils. Talk about each step as you "cook."		Play hide and seek. Encourage your child to count while you hide.				

The activities this month will focus on play to help your child prepare for school. Play is a child's work. Play provides the opportunity for children to work on language, math skills, social skills, scientific thinking, writing, pre-reading skills, and connecting to the world around them. Play helps children understand that learning is fun.

Readiness Domain Focus: Approaches to Learning; Cognitive/General Knowledge; Language and Communication; Social-Emotional Development

From *Counting Down to Kindergarten: A Complete Guide to Creating a School Readiness Program for Your Community*, R. Lynn Baker (Chicago: American Library Association, 2015).

Self-Help and Motor Skills

SELF-HELP SKILLS

Self-help skills include behaviors such as caring for one's own bathroom needs, hanging up one's own coat, and controlling one's emotions. This skill area is one of the most important indicators of school readiness according to kindergarten teachers. It is important to help children work on social skill development and adaptive skills in order to help make the transition as smooth as possible.

MOTOR SKILLS

Physical skills including large and small muscle movements are important indicators of readiness. Large muscle movements, such as running, walking, jumping, and lifting are known as gross motor movements, which contribute to a child's ability to care for his/her own needs. Fine motor skills are small muscle movements, such as pinching, grasping, squeezing, pressing, and twisting. Fine motor skills are needed for writing, cutting, buttoning, zipping, and tying—all important skills needed for kindergarten activities.

APPROACHES TO LEARNING

The way a child learns is dependent on his/her self-concept and health. Listening skills are also a part of how a child learns, and this is connected to the ability for a child to have self-control in group situations. Children learn from other children, as well. It is easier for children to focus on what the teacher is saying when they are well rested, healthy, and feel good about themselves. In order for children to acclimate to kindergarten, it is important for them to be part of a social situation with peers before kindergarten. Play dates, library programs, and other group activities help prepare children for the transition.

BOOKS THAT ENCOURAGE PHYSICAL WELL-BEING

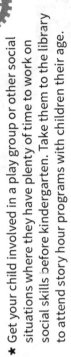

* *I Like Myself!* –Karen Beaumont; David Catrow
* *The Vegetables We Eat* –Gail Gibbons
* *Ready, Set, Skip!* –Jane O'Connor; Ann James
* *The Busy Body Book* –Julie Sykes; Tim Warnes

BOOKS THAT ENCOURAGE SELF-HELP SKILLS

* *Hands Are Not For Hitting* –Dr. Martine Agassi; Marieka Heinlen
* *Ella Sarah Gets Dressed* –Margaret Chodos-Irvine
* *It's Hard to be Five: Learning How to Work My Control Panel* –Jamie Lee Curtis
* *Llama Llama Time to Share* –Anna Dewdney
* *The Kissing Hand* –Audrey Penn; Ruth E. Harper; Nancy M. Leak

ACTIVITIES THAT ENCOURAGE MOTOR/SELF-HELP SKILLS

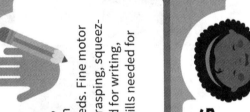

* Get your child involved in a play group or other social situations where they have plenty of time to work on social skills before kindergarten. Take them to the library to attend story hour programs with children their age.

* Take your child to the park. Encourage them to run, climb, skip, and slide. All of these activities are important to a child's physical development.

* With supervision, allow your child to use scissors to cut out pictures in a magazine. It is important for a child to have practice with scissors before kindergarten.

* Encourage your child to put on their own clothes, shoes, and jacket. Encourage your child to hang up their own jacket and put things away when they are finished. Give them a simple chore to do independently each day, such as set the table, or feed the pet.

EARLY LITERACY PRACTICE: SELF-HELP AND MOTOR SKILLS

SUNDAY	MONDAY	TUESDAY	WEDNESDAY	THURSDAY	FRIDAY	SATURDAY
		Visit the library! Encourage your child to carry some of the books they would like to check out.		Encourage your child to cut pictures from a magazine with supervision. Remind them: thumb in the top of the scissors.		Encourage your child to work on zipping their own zipper.
Hang a shirt with buttons on a hanger within reach for your child. Encourage your child to button it.	Have a "skipping" race outside to help your child practice skipping.		Unlace a pair of shoes and encourage your child to lace them back up correctly.		Encourage your child to walk up and down steps by alternating feet.	
		Visit the library! Check out books about kindergarten.		Supply large beads and pipe cleaners. Encourage your child to string the beads with supervision.		Play with play dough to help strengthen your child's hand muscles.
	Encourage your child to hang up his/her own laundry on hangers.		Play "Simon Says" focusing on physical movements.		Go to the park and run with your child.	
Practice shoe tying with your child. Model how to tie shoes by reaching around your child.		Visit the library! Check out CDs with music and movement activities.				

The activities this month will help foster your child's self-help skills. Activities that work on fine motor skills such as writing, cutting, stringing, and lacing, and large motor skills such as running and skipping, are also included.

Readiness Domain Focus: Approaches to Learning; Social-Emotional Development; Health and Physical Well-Being

From *Counting Down to Kindergarten: A Complete Guide to Creating a School Readiness Program for Your Community*, R. Lynn Baker (Chicago: American Library Association, 2015).

Copy and paste these months to use on your readiness calendar.

july

august

september

october

november

december

january

february

march

april

may

june

CHAPTER 8

EXAMPLES OF PUBLIC LIBRARY
School Readiness
PROGRAMS

IF YOUR LIBRARY HAS NOT YET DEVELOPED A SCHOOL READINESS program, now is the perfect time. The great thing about creating a program for your community now is that there are other public library systems that have already begun the journey. While this book walks you through the entire process of creating a program, you may find that there are specific characteristics of your community that you would like to address with your activities. Before you begin the planning process, take a look at this chapter to see if there are other public libraries that have already developed services that might fit your needs.

Local Community Programs

There are several state- and national-level public library programs that have been developed or are being developed in response to the current understanding of early childhood education and school readiness. Some programs concentrate more on the early literacy outcomes of participating children, while others emphasize training parents and/or caregivers in order to instill early literacy practices that can be used at home. Still other programs look at the importance of training staff first in order to improve school readiness services. In this section, we explore a few early literacy and school readiness programs that are already being offered by local public library systems.

CARROLL COUNTY PUBLIC LIBRARY, MARYLAND

In response to national school readiness goals and early childhood research, the state of Maryland developed the Maryland Model for School Readiness (MMSR) framework in 2006.[1] This framework laid out the definition of school readiness for the state, as well as the need for improving the quality of early learning experiences. Carroll County Public Library recognized the connection between early literacy services that were being provided by the public library and the needs outlined in the MMSR. In an effort to make an intentional connection for the community, the Carroll County Public Library developed the Early Literacy Training Assessment Project (ELTAP) in 2005.[2] This project assessed the impact of early literacy training for in-home childcare providers. The ELTAP library project enabled the library system to connect directly to the state's goal of improving early learning experiences for the children attending in-home care in their community.

As part of the project, the library provided research-based early literacy workshops and resources based on the Every Child Ready to Read model and resources for in-home childcare providers.[3] In order to assess the impact of the training, children attending each caregiver's program were assessed prior to the training, and once again after the caregiver completed the workshops. The results showed that there was a positive impact on the scores of the children who attended settings where the caregiver had participated in the training. The work of the Carroll County Public Library has provided evidence of what many public libraries have known for years: when adults are knowledgeable and intentionally apply early literacy knowledge and practices in their engagement with young children, it has a positive impact on the literacy development of the children. The work that was begun by the Carroll County Public Library has led to other studies across the nation. The Pierce County Library System in Washington State was one of the systems to use Carroll County Library's project as a framework for their own study.

PIERCE COUNTY LIBRARY SYSTEM, WASHINGTON STATE

The Pierce County Library System in Washington recognized the need to advocate for the early childhood services within their community. The library system was instrumental in the development of Washington's statewide Early Learning Public Library Partnership (ELPLP).[4] The library was also active in the development of the county's First 5 Fundamentals partnership in 2008, which focuses on pulling together educational institutions, health service providers, and family service organizations that provide services during the first five years of a child's development.[5] The partnership was created with the understanding that families and young children benefit from collaboration between all sectors of the early childhood community. First 5 Fundamentals partners have goals that aim to foster parent engagement and ensure high-quality child care.

In response to the library's goals and the goals of the First 5 Fundamentals partnership, the Pierce County Library System developed the Emergent Readers Literacy Training and Assessment Program in 2010.[6] As with Carroll County's project, Pierce County focused on providing early literacy training for in-home childcare providers over a six-month period, and assessed children in the programs before and after the training. The results showed a positive impact on the early literacy skills of the children who attended the settings where the caregiver had participated in the trainings, just as Carroll County's project had shown.

The Carroll County and Pierce County studies provide strong evidence of the impact public libraries can make through training in-home caregivers in early literacy. Another library system that has made a big impact on early literacy practices in the home is the Columbus Metropolitan Library in Ohio.

COLUMBUS METROPOLITAN LIBRARY, OHIO

The Columbus Metropolitan Library system established the Ready to Read Corps in 2009 in order to reach at-risk families in their homes and neighborhoods.[7] The Ready to Read Corps uses the early literacy practices of Every Child Ready to Read as its framework for outreach services and activities. The initiative was developed in response to kindergarten entrance scores showing that a large majority of children in Columbus were beginning kindergarten not ready to learn. The library responded by targeting communities with families that are statistically at-risk. Outreach programs are held in family homes, laundromats, and physicians' offices, among other places in the community. Since its inception, the Ready to Read Corps has received numerous grants and has grown to include a multilingual staff to reach families of various cultural backgrounds and languages. In-house programs are also provided at Columbus Metropolitan Library that focus on early literacy practices for families and school readiness activities for children.

While some programs focus on training childcare providers in early literacy practices, others offer early literacy and school readiness experiences for families. There are also library systems who are developing their own programs that strive to combine what the library knows about early literacy with all the other components of school readiness.

PAUL SAWYIER PUBLIC LIBRARY, FRANKFORT, KENTUCKY

Kentucky's kindergarten entrance scores showed that the majority of kindergarten children in the state were entering school not ready to learn. In response to these results, Paul Sawyier Public Library began offering the Countdown to Kindergarten program in 2013. The original program was designed for parents/caregivers and children to attend together in the spring or summer before children enter kindergarten in the fall. This book is based on the success of that original program. A set of sessions was added for parents and caregivers to attend without children in order to best facilitate direct conversation between parents/caregivers and community-based guest speakers. These adult sessions are offered one full year prior to the child entering kindergarten. By offering adult sessions in the fall and adult/child sessions in the spring, the library is able to build a yearlong relationship with the families who attend both sessions.

The adult/child program combines the best practices of the second edition of Every Child Ready to Read with state and national early childhood standards, the state indicators of school readiness, developmentally appropriate practice (see chapter one), and input from community-wide kindergarten teachers. Participants receive readiness calendars similar to the one included in chapter seven, and weekly programs include activities that are comparable to the lesson plans in chapter six. The program allows the library to collaborate with the early childhood community and to connect parents/caregivers to their services. By collaborating with schools and early childhood service providers throughout the community, the library is able to gain their support and establish buy-in. The early childhood community helps promote the program to parents, and the library promotes community services to parents. The Countdown program has helped validate public library school readiness services among other community services, and the overall success of the program has opened a discussion between libraries and the early childhood community statewide. This led to the development of a school readiness task force for Kentucky's public libraries. (We discuss the task force in the next section.)

Local programs that intentionally strive to connect early literacy practices with local needs and services—as well as strive to connect to statewide school readiness initiatives—have the greatest potential for impacting children, families, and communities.

Statewide Programs

Some of the local programs we have talked about in this chapter have led to collaborative efforts to develop and promote school readiness programs statewide. We will take a look at several statewide initiatives in this section. Just as local libraries can learn from one another to develop better services for their own communities, state systems can learn from other states. State library systems can use other state initiatives as a framework for developing their own initiatives. This ensures reliability as the most current practices are added to initiatives which have already been put into place and tested. In this section, we will take a look at several states which have developed school readiness initiatives. Many of these came about due to local public libraries leading the charge.

STATE OVERVIEW: MARYLAND

In Maryland, the state library system (the Division of Library Development and Services) exists under the state department of education. For this reason, collaboration between public libraries and educational entities is a natural partnership. While most library systems may not have the advantage of being within the same government department within their state, Maryland public libraries provide a model that other libraries can strive to accomplish with concentrated effort. Maryland's work clearly shows the importance of working closely with your state's department of education, as well as other early childhood service organizations within your state and community.

Kathleen Reif, director of St. Mary's County Library in Leonardtown, Maryland, developed and chaired the Maryland Association of Public Library Administrators (MAPLA) Birth to Four Task Force in 1998. This task force began statewide campaign and collaborative partnership with Ready at Five, an organization of the Maryland Business Roundtable for Education. Due to the work of the task force and its work with Ready at Five, public libraries are considered equal partners in the state of Maryland's school readiness initiative. In 2001, Maryland began a public awareness campaign to call attention to the importance of the first five years of life toward a child's later development in school. This campaign, known as It's Never Too Early, also advocated for the important role that libraries play in helping to prepare children for school.[8] Due to the unified effort of public libraries across the state, Maryland became the first state to appoint a public librarian to their state Governor's Early Childhood Advisory Council. The advisory council recognizes that public libraries foster early learning skills through programs and services that help prepare children for school.[9]

With the existing partnership between Maryland public libraries and the state department of education, public libraries were included as partners in the federal Early Learning Challenge Race to the Top Grant that Maryland received in 2011. Maryland's State Department of Education was awarded a grant in the amount of 50 million dollars over a four-year period. One of the objectives included in the grant was that public libraries within the state will help increase family engagement with early literacy activities.[10] Not only is the public library the perfect institution to connect with literacy, but because of its public service status, the library has the capability to reach families that other organizations may not be able to reach. This is true not only for libraries in Maryland, but for libraries across the entire country. While public libraries in other states may have to work harder to establish a partnership with their state department of education simply because such a partnership did not exist before, Maryland offers a strong road map for other libraries to follow.

STATE OVERVIEW: COLORADO

In an effort to provide the best school readiness programming possible throughout the state of Colorado, state libraries have offered early literacy training to library staff since 2004.[11] The training uses the best practices and emergent literacy skills of the first and second editions of Every Child Ready to Read as the foundational knowledge for leading early literacy programs. The Colorado Libraries for Early Literacy (CLEL) was developed in 2008 in order to train staff, promote the importance of early literacy, and advocate for the role of public libraries.[12] The committee consists of public library staff and early childhood educators who provide services to families and young children. CLEL has since become an advisory council to the Colorado State Library, providing data from early literacy programs and services from across the state. CLEL has also created an online resource for parents, Storyblocks (www.storyblocks.org).[13] This site was part of a grant that CLEL received from the Institute of Museum and Library Services. It offers video resources presented by library staff for use with infants, toddlers, and preschoolers. Each video connects to emergent literacy skills and best early literacy practices through activities such as songs, rhymes, and fingerplays. The presenter of each video explains how literacy skills are being addressed by the activity, helping parents/caregivers make connections between playing, singing, and building literacy skills.

Members of CLEL are required to serve on one of five committees: training, advocacy, communication, membership, or annual conference. There is also a steering committee, responsible for guiding the activities and plans for the group. CLEL offers an annual conference of workshops presented by state librarians and community early childhood professionals. Funding is provided for CLEL through donations made by individual libraries across the state.

STATE OVERVIEW: KENTUCKY

Public library staff from across the state of Kentucky also established a school readiness task force in 2013. The Public Library School Readiness Task Force was developed in collaboration with the Kentucky Department for Libraries and Archives.[14] The task force, now known as READiness Matters, was created in an effort to promote public libraries as school readiness service providers within the state, as well as to support programming practices through training opportunities for library staff. The task force established partnerships with representatives from the Kentucky Department of Education, the Governor's Office of Early Childhood, Northern Kentucky University, and the University of Kentucky in order to gain support and insight from each organization. Task force members serve on a voluntary basis and include library staff and directors from across the state, as well as representation from the aforementioned organizations. READiness Matters continues to advocate for public library school readiness services and has successfully secured seats on several early childhood advisory boards of the Governor's Office of Early Childhood. Public libraries are highly encouraged by the task force to join their local community early childhood councils in order to advocate for their library's school readiness services and to build partnerships with other early childhood service providers in their local communities.

Task force members are asked to serve on subcommittees that focus efforts in each of the following areas: resources and training, research and data, public awareness, and advocacy. The resources and training subcommittee seeks to share resources pertaining to school readiness, early literacy, and early childhood development with Kentucky public library staff through online tools, training opportunities, and sponsorship of regional peer mentoring groups.[15] The subcommittee also collaborates with colleges and universities, as well as professional library associations, in order to organize school readiness and early literacy training opportunities. The resources and training committee officially adopted the best practices of the second edition of Every Child Ready to Read as the foundational core of school readiness and early literacy for public library programs within the state.

The research and data subcommittee gathers and shares relevant research that supports the mission of the task force: to advocate for public library school readiness services. The subcommittee collaborates with educational institutions to help develop studies that substantiate the role of the public library, especially in connection to early literacy and state readiness data. The task force's public awareness and advocacy subcommittee works to actively promote the early literacy and school readiness programs of public libraries from across the state. This subcommittee also develops statewide promotional materials for the task force and seeks to establish collaborative relationships with organizations that might further promote public library school readiness services. The READiness Matters task force is led by a steering committee consisting of chair and cochair representatives from each of the subcommittees. The steering committee continues to be a volunteer effort, led primarily by public library staff who appreciate the need for advocacy efforts and standardized training for public libraries. READiness Matters's mission is to educate, standardize, and advance early literacy and school readiness public library services in order to better prepare children, families, schools, and communities within the state. READiness Matters also seeks to build partnerships with library systems from other states in order to promote public library school readiness services on a national level.

STATE OVERVIEW: OHIO

The Ohio Ready to Read (ORTR) task force combines the efforts of the State Library Council and the State Library of Ohio.[16] The initiative aims to promote the importance of early literacy and advocates for public library school readiness programs in their state. The task force consists of public library staff from around the state of Ohio. The ORTR task force offers resources to librarians through a website that provides lesson plans, booklists, activities, and ideas for using the second edition of Every Child Ready to Read in programs.[17] Links to other early literacy resources are also available on the website. ORTR provides an early literacy trainer, and individual library systems are able to request a free workshop on the basic practices of early literacy for their staff through ORTR.

Ohio Public Libraries collaborated with widely respected early literacy consultant, Saroj Ghoting, to debut her STAR POWER workshops for Ohio library staff in 2011. The STAR POWER program focuses on the early literacy skills and best practices of Every Child Ready to Read.[18] Because the program debuted in the state of Ohio, the ORTR task force was able to contribute content for the training, which connected directly to the needs of their state. The ORTR website offers downloadable resources from the STAR POWER training for new employees or those who were not able to attend the original training. The website also provides information as needed for libraries across the state that seek to learn more about methods for implementing early literacy practices within their programs.

STATE OVERVIEW: WISCONSIN

Wisconsin public libraries responded to the state's "New Wisconsin Promise" school readiness initiative with a statewide Library Leadership Conference in 2003. This conference helped spearhead the Early Learning Initiative for Wisconsin Public Libraries.[19] During the conference, information was presented on increasing reading readiness activities in preschool programs, brain development research findings, and grant opportunities to help libraries increase school readiness programing opportunities for patrons. Following the conference, regional trainings were offered in collaboration with early childhood professional organizations from across the state. The regional trainings concentrated on intentional programs rooted in early childhood development, early literacy development, and best practices for school readiness. The Wisconsin Department of Public Instruction received a grant from the Institute of Museum and Library Services, which enabled them to establish the Growing Wisconsin Readers initiative in 2013.[20] This initiative promotes early literacy through an informational website for caregivers and parents about the importance of reading to children. The website also provides resources for librarians working with children before kindergarten, including links to research and articles, printable brochures for use with parents, and free resources from early literacy trainings. The site offers a convenient way for libraries to connect to information as needed in order to build stronger early literacy/school readiness programs for their communities.

STATE OVERVIEW: VIRGINIA

The State Library of Virginia, with assistance from a grant from the Institute of Museum and Library Services (IMLS), created an early literacy program that includes a family literacy calendar for parents and caregivers. The calendar, Day-ByDayVA, is based on a calendar developed by South Carolina State Library, and is accessible online for use by parents/caregivers.[21] The calendar and logos are available for public libraries within the state to link to within their local websites and newsletters. Early Literacy Activity Centers are provided for one hundred libraries within the state with help from the IMLS grant. The activity centers include materials to foster active play and language development between adults and children in the library. The Library of Virginia also sponsors early literacy trainings for library staff, and offers online video tutorials which address readiness skills. The videos provide examples of verbal asides to use with parents during school readiness programs. Saroj Ghoting provided many of the videos for this project, which can be accessed on the Library of Virginia website.[22] The state library also offers online early literacy and school readiness training for Virginia library staff, as well as face-to-face trainings.

National Program: Family Place Libraries

While there are some individual systems developing school readiness programs—and several statewide school readiness initiatives being developed in response to state-level focus on the importance of early childhood—there are also programs being developed on a national level. These programs are often based on successful local and statewide programs.

One such program is Family Place Libraries. This initiative was established in 1996, based on the Middle Country (New York) Public Library parent/child early childhood workshop model.[23] The goal of Family Place Libraries is to promote public libraries as community centers for parents and young children. The parent/child workshop, which was a part of the original model, remains at the core of services provided by Family Place Libraries.

Today, there are over 250 Family Place Libraries in the United States, in nearly thirty states. Programs vary among participating libraries, but the services offered at these libraries are all focused on engaging parents/caregivers and children in activities which foster early literacy skills. Play areas are built into the children's area in many Family Place Libraries because play between adults and children is valued for its role in fostering language and literacy development. The websites of participating libraries also offer literacy tips and activities for parents to do with their children at home.

The initiative offers training to participating public libraries through a three-day face-to-face institute and continuing online workshops.[24] Libraries interested in becoming one of the Family Place Libraries are required to send a librarian to the Family Place Training Institute, which is scheduled each year at the model library, Middle Country Public Library, located in New York. Training is provided in such areas as community outreach, child development, emergent literacy, and developing partnerships that support services to families and children.

Intentionality in Programming

One thing you may notice from the examples in this chapter is a strong focus on early literacy as the foundation of public library programs for preschool children and families. While it is natural that the public library should establish itself as a literacy authority within its own community and state, it is also important to note that it is equally natural for public library programs to foster other school readiness skills in addition to early literacy. This is something that the public library must be intentional about—both in the training of its staff and in the advocacy of its programs and services. Without intentionality, early childhood public library programs are still enjoyable, but there are so many other things that can be a part of the fun. There is no need to remove the enjoyment from activities in order to turn a preschool storyhour session into a school readiness program. The difference exists in the intention behind the activities that are chosen.

When a local school readiness program is successfully received by patrons—and the local early childhood community—the next significant step is to share its success on a statewide level. There are many local public library programs that have made a state and nationwide impact because they were shared with other libraries and early childhood service providers. Do not keep your successes to yourself when your program might make an impact on other communities. Public libraries will have the most influence on school readiness efforts when we learn to be intentional in our program delivery, in our advocacy efforts, and in our willingness to share with one another.

Notes

1. Maryland Model for School Readiness, accessed January 2015, www.mdk 12.org/instruction/ensure/mmsr/MMSRpkFrameworkAndStandards.pdf.

2. Elaine M. Czarnecki, "A Report of: The Carroll County Public Library Emergent Literacy Training Assessment Project," August 2006, http://library.carr.org/about/docs/emlitreport.pdf.

3. Dorothy Stoltz, Elaine M. Czarnecki, and Connie Wilson, *Every Child Ready for School: Helping Adults Inspire Young Children to Learn* (Chicago: American Library Association, 2013).

4. Early Learning Public Library Partnership, accessed January 2015, http://earlylearning.org/about-us/early-learning-public-library-partnership.

5. First 5 Fundamentals of Pierce County, accessed January 2015, www.first5 fundamentals.org/.

6. Eliza Dresang, "Pierce County Library System Emergent Readers Literacy Training and Assessment Program Research Report," accessed January 2015, www.piercecountylibrary.org/files/library/research-report.pdf.

7. Kathy Shahbodaghi, "Taking Ready to Read outside the Library and into the Community," Ready to Read Ohio, April 2010, www.library.ohio.gov/marketing/Newsletters/TheNews/2010/April/Ready2ReadOutsideCML.

8. S. M. Shauck, "Maryland Public Libraries: It's Never Too Early," *Journal of Youth Services in Libraries* 15, no. 2 (2002): 9–14.

9. Maryland Early Childhood Advisory Council, "What Success Looks Like: Three-Year Action Plan, 2009–2012," accessed January 2015, www.maryland publicschools.org/NR/rdonlyres/28B75D91-0DCF-4B6F-92CB-E21A6A 638486/21158/ECAC3year.pdf.

10. Maryland State Department of Education, "Race to the Top Early Learning Challenge Grant," accessed January 2015, www.marylandpublicschools.org/MSDE/divisions/child_care/challenge/.

11. Library Research Service, "Colorado Public Libraries Help Children Get Ready to Read," May 22, 2008, www.lrs.org/fast-facts-reports/colorado-public-libraries-help-children-get-ready-to-read/.

12. Colorado Libraries for Early Literacy, www.clel.org.

13. Songs and Rhymes That Build Readers, www.storyblocks.org.

14. Kentucky Education and Workforce Development Cabinet, "Task Force Formed to Promote Early Literacy, School Readiness Programs at Kentucky's Public Libraries" (press release), December 20, 2013, http://educationcabinet .ky.gov/newsroom/pressreleases/literacytaskforce2013.htm.

15. READiness Matters!, http://readinessmatterskentucky.weebly.com.

16. Ohio Ready to Read, www.ohreadytoread.org.

17. Ohio Ready to Read, "Early Literacy Resources," accessed January 2015, www.ohreadytoread.org/earlyliteracyresources.html.

18. See STAR POWER workshops, www.earlylit.net/star-power.

19. Barbara Huntington, "Early Learning Initiative for Wisconsin Public Libraries," 2005, http://pld.dpi.wi.gov/sites/default/files/imce/pld/pdf/earlylearning.pdf.

20. Growing Wisconsin Readers, accessed January 2015, http://growingwisconsin readers.org/home.

21. DaybyDayVA, accessed January 2015, www.daybydayva.org.

22. Library of Virginia, "Early Literacy: Early Literacy Videos," accessed January 2015, www.lva.virginia.gov/lib-edu/ldnd/early-literacy.

23. Middle County Public Library, "Family Place Libraries," accessed January 2015, www.middlecountrypubliclibrary.org/children/early-childhood/family-place -libraries.

24. See Family Place Training Institute, http://familyplacelibraries.org/training .html.

PLANNING A FALL SESSION
for Adults

THIS CHAPTER PROVIDES LESSON PLANS FOR A SIX-WEEK session of programs for adults to attend without children. The ideal time of year to offer this session is in the fall, one year prior to the child entering kindergarten. As mentioned earlier, offering the adult sessions in the fall enables you to begin a relationship with families earlier—and hopefully for a longer duration—as children prepare for kindergarten over the next year. Inviting community experts to come speak during sessions with adults only offers parents/caregivers the ability to better connect with the speakers that you schedule.

Preparing for Your Program

During registration, ask adults to complete the parent questionnaire (see figure 4.1). The questionnaire can help you determine which community guest speakers to invite to your program, matching the needs of your participants. Making the questionnaire available during registration will provide plenty of time for you to contact your speakers and schedule each of them to correspond with your lesson plans. By scheduling in advance, you will also be able to announce the guests for each session of the program prior to their session. This helps participants know what to expect each session, and can help you as you promote your program. A list of suggested guest speakers can be found in chapter five; however, there are many possibilities, depending on the needs of parents/caregivers who register for your program.

In the event that your library must allow children to attend this program, it is helpful if you are able to have another staff member prepare a separate program for the children in another area of the library away from the adult session. This way, the adults will be free to interact with one another and with the speaker each week. If you offer a single session with guest speakers and children attending the session in the same room, you can prepare "quiet bags" with activities to engage children in quiet, hands-on activities during the guest-speaker portion of the program. To make the bags prior to the session, use large (one to one-and-a-half gallon) zip-top bags with items that can be quietly and independently explored by children on their own. Supplies for quiet bags may include items such as:

- Pipe cleaners and pony beads (children can string the beads onto pipe cleaners)
- Crayons and small pads of paper
- Small magnetic drawing boards (such as Magna Doodle)
- Wikki Stix (multicolored, wax-covered strings that can be bent into shapes)
- Felt boards (made with felt glued to small pieces of cardboard) and shapes cut from colorful felt for children to place onto the boards
- Lacing cards made from laminated shapes with holes punched through them; provide yarn or shoelaces for children to lace around the shapes.
- Stickers and laminated paper (so that the stickers will be repositionable)
- Small wipe-off boards and dry-erase markers with eraser tops
- Magnetic wands and small pieces of pipe cleaners

You should offer the bags to children as they enter the room, and explain to the adults that the children can use the activities in the bags while the guest speakers are talking with the adults. If you use items that do not have to be used again, you can allow the children to take them home with them at the end of the session. If you have items that need to be collected and used again, be sure to collect the bags at the door at the end of the session, and have something that can be given to the child in exchange—such as a sticker, die-cut, or pencil. This will help children who may have difficulty returning items before leaving.

Duration

Plan your program schedule, but remember to keep program plans flexible enough to change as needed according to any interests, questions, or concerns that may arise. Allot approximately thirty minutes per session for speakers and discussion, and an additional thirty minutes for completing hands-on projects each week. (We will cover specific ideas for hands-on activities in the lesson plan section of this chapter.) Just as with your readiness program for adults and children to attend together, you may choose to offer the program for adults in a six-week session or as a larger onetime event, depending on the interest and needs of your community.

If you choose to offer the adult session as a onetime event, you may decide to invite several different types of speakers as guests and offer the program as a school readiness fair with guests seated at tables around the room. One additional option for this type of program is to introduce the session as a "community roundtable" type of program, in which guests sit alongside parents/caregivers and have an open discussion. This type of program can also be offered prior to the start of the full six-week program as a single kickoff session. Use the opportunity to share information with parents about the upcoming sessions. A large, onetime event allows you to connect adults with other early childhood services in your community, and it provides the opportunity to promote your lengthier programs to the adults who attend.

Planning Topics and Activities

By focusing each one of your sessions on the early literacy practices of Every Child Ready to Read and aligning your family calendar accordingly, your program will offer consistent information. Aligning special guests with the interests of your participants and connecting the schedule to your readiness calendar will help you create a fall semester program for adults that will carry over nicely into your spring sessions for children and adults.

Literacy Tool Stations

In order to provide hands-on, practical tools and information for the adults attending your program, create "literacy tool stations." These stations should include take-home information, checklists, resource lists, and/or specific school readiness products for adults to actively try. The resources and tools offered at the stations each week should correspond with the Every Child Ready to Read practice and school readiness domain focus of the session, if possible. The lesson plans in this section of the book include ideas, suggestions, and online links for finding specific literacy tools for parents/caregivers each week.

Hands-On Projects: Countdown Boxes

Your session for adults should also incorporate crafts, allowing adults to create school readiness take-home projects for their children each week. The lesson plans included in this chapter include suggestions for crafts to offer each session. During the first week, adults will choose and decorate "Countdown Boxes," which are plastic shoe boxes that are decorated by the adults to hold the readiness activities they create for their children each week. The intention is that adult participants will add their take-home projects to the boxes at home over the course of the six weeks. The handcrafted take-home projects should connect to the literacy practices and readiness skills that you introduce each week. Boxes can be decorated with items such as stickers, foam die-cuts, ribbon, or paste jewels.

Lesson Plans for Adult Sessions

The lesson plans that follow are based on the framework of the Countdown to Kindergarten program, which is the program model for this book. The lesson plans include specific components, which correspond with the family calendar and the adult/child lesson plans in this book. The structure of the sessions includes: an overview to share with adults about the literacy practice and readiness skill focus each week; ideas for possible guest speakers; suggestions for handouts; ideas for creating "literacy tool stations"; and hands-on crafts for adults to create for their child's "Countdown Box." Guest speakers should coincide with the topics each week; however, your program should be flexible enough to shift as needed.

The outline of the skills and practices covered each week corresponds with the lesson plan outline for the adult/child sessions (found in chapter six):

Lesson Plan week 1/Literacy Calendar month 1: **Talking**

Lesson Plan week 2/Literacy Calendar month 2: **Singing**

Lesson Plan week 3/Literacy Calendar month 3: **Reading**

Lesson Plan week 4/Literacy Calendar month 4: **Writing**

Lesson Plan week 5/Literacy Calendar month 5: **Playing**

Lesson Plan week 6/Literacy Calendar month 6: **Self-Help/Motor Skills**

LESSON PLAN: WEEK 1

ECRR practice: Talking
Readiness domain focus: Social-emotional development, language and communication development

Introduction to the Program

Introduce yourself and ask adult participants to introduce themselves to the rest of the group. Introduce the concept of the program and briefly describe the adult/child sessions that will take place the following spring. Explain that this current program is meant for adults to attend without children in order for the adults to better connect with one another and with guest speakers. Provide any introductory handouts which you have prepared regarding the Every Child Ready to Read practices, early literacy skills, and/or school readiness indicators. Explain the structure and schedule of the program, and describe the literacy tool and craft stations that will be set up in the room each week. Remind the participants to complete the questionnaire (figure 4.1) if they have not already done so, as this will help you plan guest speakers and activities for the remainder of the sessions. Also, take the time to discuss your state's definition of school readiness and the entrance screening tool that your state uses (if your state uses one). Explain the five fundamental domains of school readiness (from chapter three) and how your program will help the participants foster each one with their child at home.

Overview of the Week's Literacy Practice: Talking

Explain that the literacy skill focus of the first session is the skill of talking. You might say to the group: "Talking is an important skill for children, as it helps to develop narrative language, vocabulary, and communication skills, which are important for literacy development. The more words a child hears throughout the day, the more words they will speak and know—and this helps with reading. In this session, we will discuss some strategies for developing language and communication skills through experiences that encourage talking."

Overview of the Week's Readiness Skills:
Social-Emotional Development, Language Development

Explain that you will also be focusing on two readiness skills this week: social-emotional development and language and communication development. Share the following with the group: "We will also take a look at the important role that social skills play in making a successful transition into kindergarten. It is important for young children to be around other children in order to develop social skills which help them to express their thoughts, needs, and regulate their own emotions. Taking turns, sharing, and being able to control one's emotions are also important social skills for young children to develop before kindergarten."

Guest speaker suggestions: Speech therapist; preschool teacher; developmental interventionist; previous parent attendee of your school readiness program

Suggestions for handouts: Distribute the "Week 1: Talking" handout at the end of this chapter (handout 9.1). You may find additional information to distribute regarding language and communication at the following sites:

- The Hanen Centre (www.hanen.org) offers information and tips for promoting language, and literacy.
- Parenting Counts (www.parentingcounts.org) provides a developmental timeline on their website that is divided into specific domains, including communication.
- Chateau Meddybemps Parent's Guide (www.meddybemps.com) offers suggestions for skill-building activities for parents, divided into several developmental skill areas.

Countdown Box Craft Project: Decorate Countdown Boxes
Provide plastic shoe boxes with lids for each participant to create a Countdown Box for their child. Supply pieces of colorful felt, and encourage participants to create a felt board on the inside of the lid by attaching it to the inside of the lid with a hot glue gun. Supply additional felt for participants to create shapes to be used on the felt board. If you have a die-cut machine available for use, you may want to allow participants to cut out letters and/or shapes using the die-cut machine. Explain to participants that they should encourage their children to create stories at home using the felt board. You should also supply items such as letter stickers, foam die-cuts, ribbon, and paste jewels for your participants to decorate the outside of the boxes. Explain that you will be creating new activities each week of the program to be added to the Countdown Boxes at home.

Literacy Tool Spotlight:
"Get Ready to Read: Transitioning to Kindergarten Toolkit"
This downloadable and printable toolkit includes information about early literacy and school readiness indicators.[1] It includes a printable screening tool for parents to use to help them determine if their child is ready to learn. Instructions for administering and scoring the screening tool is also provided. Skill-building activities and printable activity cards are included with the toolkit as well.

LESSON PLAN: WEEK 2

ECRR practice: Singing

Readiness domain focus: Approaches to learning, social-emotional development language development

Overview of the Week's Literacy Practice: Singing

Introduce the important role that singing plays toward language development. Share the following with the group: "Singing slows down the sounds in words, which helps children understand the concept that words are made up of individual sounds. Singing and music can also help children retain what they have learned. The rhythm of music can help a child understand the rhythm of language and connect them better to what they are learning."

Overview of the Week's Readiness Skills: Approaches to Learning, Social-Emotional Development, Language Development

Introduce the connection that music has with the week's readiness skills. Share the following with the group: "Music and movement can help evoke interest in learning among young children. Music-based activities and group songs encourage young children to relate to peers in the group, as well as to express themselves verbally."

Guest speaker suggestions for the week: Music teacher from a local elementary school; Kindermusik teacher; speech therapist

Suggestions for handouts: Distribute the "Week 2: Singing" handout (handout 9.2). You may find additional information to distribute regarding language and communication at the following sites:

- Kindermusik (www.kindermusik.com) is a music and movement educational program for young children and families. Trained consultants own their own businesses and provide classes in various locations. Many are willing to offer a onetime class at the library. The Kindermusik website offers research and resources.
- Let's Play Music (www.letsplaykidsmusic.com) is a blog with free resources, activities, and songs. The music is appropriate for parents/caregivers to use at home, and is also appropriate for use in the classroom or library setting. The site provides printable patterns for creating fingerpuppets and other supplemental materials for use with songs.

Countdown Box Craft Project: Shaker Eggs

Provide plastic eggs, rice and/or dried beans, colorful electrical tape, and stickers for decoration. Encourage adults to create shaker eggs for their children by filling the plastic eggs with rice or beans, and taping the plastic eggs closed with the electrical tape. Encourage participants to choose stickers to take home for their child to decorate their own shaker eggs. The shaker eggs should be added to their Countdown Boxes and used at home to facilitate singing, rhythm, and rhymes—all of which are important practice for developing reading skills.

Literacy Tool Station: Using Apps and Technology-based Tools

Offer adult program participants hands-on practice with apps on tablets or laptops, if your library has these tools for patron use. If not, you may want to offer time on your library's computers at the end of the session. Be sure to spotlight any music-based services your library offers, such as downloadable music and audio CDs. Here are a few free and low-cost apps that you may want to feature at your station this week:

- Kindermusik Radio App (www.kindermusik.com/community/mobile-apps-for-kids/) provides music with lyrics for engaging in music and movement activities at home. This app is available at low cost through iTunes.
- Starfall.com (www.starfall.com/index.htm) is a free phonics-based website that uses music and games to encourage literacy skill development. Content is provided for children in preschool through second grade.
- Mother Goose on the Loose (www.mgol.net/about/mgol-and-technology/mgol-app/) is an early literacy program which engages adults and children in activities that connect early literacy skills, music, and movement. Mother Goose on the Loose has developed a Felt Board app in which children can interact with objects on the screen which look like feltboard pieces. The children can also sing along with songs and tap along to rhythms as they play. The Mother Goose on the Loose app is available through iTunes for free.
- The Fred Rogers Center's Early Learning Environment (Ele; http://ele.fredrogerscenter.org/) is an online resource for adults looking for early learning digital resources to use with preschool children. The online resource is free of charge, and links users to suggestions, activities, videos, games, apps, and more.

LESSON PLAN: WEEK 3

ECRR practice: Reading

Readiness domain focus: Approaches to learning, social-emotional development, language development

Overview of the Week's Literacy Practice: Reading

Introduce the importance of prereading skills to the adults in your program. Share the following with the group: "Research has shown that it is important for parents/caregivers to read to their children at least twenty minutes every day. It is also important to point out familiar signs and logos—known as environmental print—in the natural context of daily life. Recognition of these types of print is often a child's first step toward reading. It is important to point out other printed text as you move through your daily routine. This helps your child generalize the knowledge that all print has meaning."

Overview of the Week's Readiness Skills: Approaches to Learning, Language Development

Describe the new school readiness indicator that you will be focusing on in this session, approaches to learning. Share the following with the group: "The term 'approaches to learning' refers to the way children feel about learning, how they enter into new situations, and if they are interested in learning new concepts. This can apply to learning individually or in a group setting. Learning in a group setting also fosters social and emotional skills that are important for kindergarten."

Guest speaker suggestions for the week: Reading specialist; parent-involvement specialist

Suggestions for handouts: Distribute the "Week 3: Reading" handout (handout 9.3). You may find additional information to distribute regarding reading at the following sites:

- Reach Out and Read Milestones of Early Literacy Development (www .reachoutandread.org/FileRepository/RORmilestones_English.pdf) is a nonprofit organization that partners with doctors to distribute books to families with young children. The site also offers information on early literacy milestones.
- Reading Is Fundamental (RIF; www.rif.org/us/literacy-resources/ articles/raising-readers.htm) offers free, downloadable, printable brochures with information to help families foster reading habits at home.

- The Home Literacy Environment Checklist provided by Get Ready to Read (www.getreadytoread.org) helps parents assess the literacy-friendliness of their home to help ensure a literacy-rich environment.

Countdown Box Craft Project: A Book about Taking Care of Books

Provide colored construction paper, white copy paper, and staplers for creating small books. Encourage adult participants to create the pages of a book by folding the white paper in half. Participants should create a front and back cover by cutting a piece of colored construction paper in half. Provide staplers for participants to staple their books together along the edge of the book. Supply the following steps for taking care of books, which adults should write on the pages of their child's book:

- When looking at a book, hold it right side up.
- Open the cover of the book from the bottom corner.
- Look at (or read) the pages of the book in order—from the left to the right.
- Turn the pages of the book from the top right-hand corner, and slowly turn the pages to the left, until you are finished.
- Put the book away when you are finished reading it.

The adults can write each step on a page of the book and illustrate the book—or leave the illustrations for their child to complete at home. Have them add the "Book about Taking Care of Books" to their child's Countdown Box at home, and to encourage their children to read the book with an adult, practicing the skills as they handle the book.

Literacy Tool Station: Hooked on Phonics

If your library has a set of Hooked on Phonics materials, place them at the station for adults to look through.[2] Other options for this station might include any phonics materials that your library has available for patron use (such as Bob Books).[3] If your library does not have any phonics sets for patron use in the collection, another option is to supply handouts about how they might obtain Hooked on Phonics sets on their own and/or information about using materials online.

LESSON PLAN: WEEK 4

ECRR practice: Writing

Readiness domain focus: Cognition and general knowledge, physical well-being and motor development, language development

Overview of the Week's Literacy Practice: Writing

Introduce writing as this week's literacy practice focus. Share the following with the group: "Early writing skills are built on a child's ability to draw or color. Early literacy skills and writing go hand in hand, as prewriting skills also help a child understand that printed letters make up words. Fine motor development and hand strength are needed in order for a child to develop writing skills."

Overview of the Week's Readiness Skills: Cognition and General Knowledge, Physical Well-Being and Motor Development, Language Development

Discuss how cognitive skills and writing skills complement one another. Share the following with the group: "As a child's cognitive abilities grow, his or her ability to connect drawings to words develops. Drawings and scribbling are part of a young child's way of communicating before he or she can actually read or write. It is important for children to have the proper tools at home in order to express their thoughts through drawing and prewriting skills. These can include tools such as pencils, pens, markers, chalk, crayons, and paint. Another important skill that is developed through writing and drawing is the fine motor control that the young child develops through learning to hold a writing utensil. This contributes to the young child's physical development."

Guest speaker suggestions for the week: A parent of a current kindergarten student (previous school readiness program attendee); art teacher; school-based occupational therapist

Suggestions for handouts: Distribute the "Week 4: Writing" handout (handout 9.4). You may find additional information to distribute regarding reading at the following sites:

- Handwriting without Tears (www.hwtears.com/hwt/parents) provides a free light version of their worksheet maker, through which adults are able to type text and print practice pages for their child. Printable letter formation charts are also available.

- Draw Your World (www.drawyourworld.com/blog/hold-the-pencil.html) offers printable handouts with the steps for proper pencil grip. Tools are also available through the website to help children develop a proper tripod pencil grip.
- Dr. Jean Feldman (www.drjean.org) offers free prewriting and beginning writing activities on her site.

Countdown Box Craft Project:
Handmade Wipe-Off Board and Dry Erase Marker

Provide lined wide-ruled writing paper and either a small laminator with film, clear contact paper, or a clear plastic sheet protector. Instead of lined paper, you can supply lined sentence strips. Encourage adult participants to laminate the lined paper or sentence strip, or place it in a sheet protector. Supply dry-erase markers and pom-poms. Provide hot-glue guns for adults to attach pom-poms to marker lids to create dry erasers on top of the markers. Adults should take the handmade dry-erase boards and erasers home to be added to their child's Countdown Box. Children can use the dry-erase boards to practice writing their name and/or letters and numbers.

Literacy Tool Spotlight:
Get Ready for School Assessment and Observation Checklist available through Handwriting without Tears

The assessment and observation checklist is available free of charge on the Handwriting without Tears website.[4] Provide copies of the checklist at the literacy tool station this week. Participants can read through the checklist during the session in order to ask any questions that they might have, and then take it home to complete with their children. The checklist will help adults to document the date when their child is able to demonstrate each language and literacy characteristic as they prepare for kindergarten. This provides a record of developmental milestones for parents and caregivers.

LESSON PLAN: WEEK 5

ECRR practice: Playing

Readiness domain focus: Approaches to learning, cognition and general knowledge, social-emotional development, language development

Overview of the Week's Literacy Practice: Playing

Introduce the importance of play to a child's development. Share the following with the group: "Play contributes to a child's developmental growth across all domains of learning. It enables a child to gain social skills through learning to share, taking turns, and getting along with others. Play should also provide opportunities for exposure to print and opportunities for writing as much as possible in order to help a child develop pre-reading skills. Dramatic (pretend) play helps children learn about the world around them, applying previous knowledge to new experiences."

Overview of the Week's Readiness Skills:
Approaches to Learning, Cognition and General Knowledge, Social-Emotional Development, Language Development

Introduce the idea that play allows children to learn while also having fun. Share the following with the group: "When learning seems fun, children are more likely to seek out opportunities to learn new things. Play also allows children to experiment with things in their world, and to learn from the outcomes of their experiments. When children are engaged in play with others, they have the opportunity to practice and develop language and communication skills. Playing with peers helps children to develop social and emotional skills that are important for starting school as well."

Guest speaker suggestions for the week: School counselor; family resource specialist

Suggestions for handouts: Distribute the "Week 5: Playing" handout (handout 9.5). You may find additional information to distribute regarding the importance of play at the following sites:

- NAEYC (National Association for the Education of Young Children; www.naeyc.org) offers brochures about the importance of play. Brochures are low cost to order, and discounts are available for large orders and/or members of NAEYC.

- Bright Horizons Family Solutions (www.brighthorizons.com) is an international childcare organization. The organization offers free parent resources on their website, which provides helpful information on the importance of play.
- Scholastic for Parents (www.scholastic.com/parents) offers information about all areas of child development, including the importance of dramatic play. Articles are available online and can be printed to distribute as handouts.

Countdown Box Craft Project: Grocery Store Kit

Provide materials for adults to create a mini grocery store for their child's Countdown Box. There are many places to find free printable price tags, store signs, coupons, and grocery lists online. Print out these items and encourage adult participants to cut them out to be added to their child's grocery store dramatic play kit. You can also provide preprinted images of fruits, vegetables, and other items found at the grocery store for adults to add to their child's mini grocery store kit. There are also printable pretend checks and money online to add to the kits. Encourage parents to save paper credit cards that come in the mail and use those with the grocery kits at home. Provide a small paper lunch sack for participants to add all the pieces to their kit to be kept in their child's Countdown Box.

Literacy Tool Station: Dramatic-Play Prop Boxes

Create a few dramatic-play prop boxes and display them at your Literacy Tool interactive station this week. Unused pizza boxes and shirt boxes can be used as prop boxes. Add things to your prop boxes and provide a printed list of ideas for other prop boxes. Here are a few suggestions for simple and easy to create prop boxes that you may want to display at the Literacy Tool station this week:

- **Pizza parlor:** Cut out a tan colored circle from felt for the pizza dough; a red piece for the sauce; small pieces of green peppers; gray pieces for mushrooms; brown pieces for meat; small red circles for pepperoni; and so on. Provide yellow yarn for the cheese. Include an apron, and plates, napkins, plastic forks, and cups. Print out and laminate a pizza menu. You may want to create your own menus with sizes, prices, and toppings.
- **Vet clinic:** Provide stuffed animals, bandages, medicine syringes, a stethoscope and gloves. Also include clipboards, paper, a pen, and file folders for children to use for keeping records and charts on the animals. A pretend x-ray can be made by printing an image of an x-ray (found online) onto a printable transparency sheet.

- **Bakery:** Include baking pans, a chef's hat, plastic rolling pin, cookie cutters, and felt circles in the shape of cookies, cakes, and doughnuts. Provide cookbooks, or create cookbooks by cutting out magazine pictures (or printing out pictures) and gluing them to paper. Add printed directions to the recipe on each page. Slide the pages into page protectors and add them to a three-ring binder in order to create a cookbook.

LESSON PLAN: WEEK 6

ECRR practice: Self-help and motor skills
Readiness domain focus: Approaches to learning, Social-emotional development, Physical Well-Being and Motor Development

Overview of the Week's Readiness Skills: Self-Help and Motor Skills

The last session of the program for adults focuses on two skills that are often identified by kindergarten teachers as the most important readiness skills. Share the following with the group: "Self-help skills refer to activities that children learn to do for themselves in order to take care of their own needs. This includes activities such as a child caring for his or her own bathroom habits, hanging up his or her own coat, and buttoning or zipping clothing."

"Motor skills include large and small muscle movements. Large motor skills refer to big muscle movements, such as running and jumping, while small motor skills include small movements, such as writing and cutting. Most self-help skills are usually reliant on a child's physical abilities and motor skill development."

Guest speaker suggestion for the week: Kindergarten teachers

Suggestions for handouts: Distribute the "Week 6: Self-Help and Motor Skills" handout (handout 9.6). You may find additional information to distribute regarding self-help and motor skills at the following sites:

- The University of Wisconsin-Extension (http://fyi.uwex.edu/parenting thepreschooler/fact-sheets) provides free fact sheets on early childhood development on their website. Parenting the Preschooler fact sheets provide information and tips for parents across developmental areas, including the development of self-help skills.
- KidsLearningStation.com (www.kidslearningstation.com/fine-motor -skills) offers free printable worksheets for tracing and cutting. These worksheets provide practice tracing and cutting a sequence of lines in order to develop stronger fine motor skills.

- Parents.com (www.parents.com/kids/printables/chore-charts/say-yes
  -to-chores/) offers tips for age-appropriate chores around the house.
  The site offers free, printable chore charts for parents to do at home with
  their children. Assigning age-appropriate household jobs with small
  children allows them to develop an understanding of personal responsibility (such as hanging up their own jacket and putting away toys).

Countdown Box Craft Project: Hand-Strengthening Activities

It is important for children to strengthen the hand muscles needed for fine
motor activities such as cutting and writing. This week, supply materials for
adult participants to create several hand strengthening activities for their child's
Countdown Box.

- **Balloon squeeze ball:** Provide well-made colorful round balloons, play
  dough, funnels, and thin wooden craft sticks or dowel rods. Instruct
  participants to attach a balloon to a funnel. Participants will roll the
  play dough into long, snakelike pieces and push the play dough into
  the balloon through the attached funnel. If needed, wooden craft sticks
  can be used to gently push the play dough through the opening of the
  funnel into the balloon. Participants continue the process until their
  balloon begins to become round, and then tie off the balloon to create
  a squeezable ball. Encourage children to squeeze the stuffed balloon in
  order to help develop hand muscles.
- **Tongs and cotton balls:** Provide plastic tongs and cotton balls for children to practice the pinching skills that are needed for developing a
  correct pencil grasp. Inexpensive plastic tongs can be purchased in a
  variety of sizes or you might want to offer plastic tweezers for developing smaller muscle strength.
- **Pipe-cleaner bracelets:** Provide pipe cleaners and pony beads. Have
  adults choose a couple of pipe cleaners and several pony beads to place
  in a small zip-top bag for their child's Countdown Box. Adults can
  encourage children to string the pony beads onto the pipe cleaners to
  create bracelets. (Stringing beads develops a pincher grasp, which helps
  with proper pencil grasp.)

Literacy Tool Station: Manual-Dexterity Boards

Create manual-dexterity boards for adult participants to take a look at during the
session. These can be used again later with children during your spring session.
These boards provide practice with buttoning, zipping, and snapping, and should
be easy for most parents to replicate for use at home. Premade dexterity boards
can also be purchased from school supply stores, but are much more costly.

- **Button board:** Hand-sew plastic buttons onto fabric and attach the fabric onto a small piece of cardboard using a hot-glue gun. Cut out felt shapes slightly larger than the buttons. Cut a slit in each shape so that children can fasten shapes onto the buttons in order to practice buttoning skills.
- **Zipper board:** Hot-glue fabric onto a piece of cardboard. Attach two pieces of felt along the outer edges of the cardboard so that the two pieces of felt come together in the center of the cardboard. Sew a zipper onto the two pieces of felt so that children can zip the pieces of felt together.
- **Snap board:** Hot-glue fabric onto a piece of cardboard. Attach two pieces of felt along the outer edges of the cardboard so that the two pieces of felt come together in the center of board, like the zipper board described above. Attach snaps to the two sides of the felt so that they snap together in the center.

At the close of your sessions for adults, be sure to provide information about the spring sessions for adults and children to attend together. As the spring registration date approaches, send a reminder e-mail to the adults who attended the fall session for adults. The goal of your readiness program is to create relationships with as many families as possible, and to continue working with as many of them as possible over the course of the entire year. Your program will have the most impact on families that you successfully create ongoing relationships with over time. When you are intentional in your efforts to seek out families, model best practices, and connect families to information and community resources that help them prepare their children for school, your program will make the most difference to your community.

Notes

1. Get Ready to Read Transitioning to Kindergarten Toolkit, accessed January 2015, www.getreadytoread.org/transition-kindergarten-toolkit/print-the-toolkit.

2. Hooked on Phonics, accessed January 2015, https://www.hookedonphonics.com.

3. Bob Books, accessed January 2015, http://bobbooks.com.

4. Get Ready for School Assessment and Observation Checklist available through Handwriting without Tears, accessed January 2015, www.hwtears.com/gss/prek-assessment/main.

Week 1: Talking

Talking with your child now is important to your child's success in school. Studies show that the more words a young child hears at home, the more success they will have in learning to read.

How to help your child now:

- Buy an echo microphone (look at the dollar store for these) and encourage your child to tell stories or sing into it.
- Sing songs with words that begin with the same sound repeated throughout.

There is a connection between natural conversation now and reading later.

How to help your child now:

- Ask questions about the pictures and the story while you read together.
- Identify objects and words as you play together.
- Read wordless books together— ask your child to tell the story by looking at the pictures.
- Talk about items at the grocery store as you shop together.
- Make up stories together.
- **Make it fun!**

Books that encourage language and vocabulary development:

- *Bark, George* by Jules Feiffer
- *Pete the Cat: I Love My White Shoes* by Eric Litwin
- *If You Give a Mouse a Cookie* by Laura Numeroff
- *Bee & Bird* by Craig Frazier

HANDOUT 9.1 From *Counting Down to Kindergarten: A Complete Guide to Creating a School Readiness Program for Your Community,* R. Lynn Baker (Chicago: American Library Association, 2015).

Week 2: Singing

Singing helps children hear the distinct sounds that make up words. Studies show that singing helps develop sound awareness, which helps children learn to read.

How to help your child now:

- Sing songs with silly words.
- Check out CDs from the library.
- Make up new words to familiar tunes, such as "Twinkle, Twinkle, Little Star."
- Check out books that are based on songs and read/sing them together with your child.

There is a connection between identifying words that rhyme and reading!

How to help your child now:

- Play a rhyming game—say a word and see if your child can come up with words that rhyme.
- Read books that have lots of rhyme, such as Dr. Seuss books.
- Play a game that break words into parts and clap as you say each syllable of a word. Have your child come up with the next word and clap the syllables.

Books that encourage singing and language development:

- *Over in the Meadow* by John M. Langstaff
- *If You're Happy and You Know It* by Jane Cabrera
- *Shake Your Sillies Out* by Raffi

Great music that promotes early literacy development:

- Laurie Berkner Band, "Bumblebee (Buzz Buzz)"; "Victor Vito"; "We Are the Dinosaurs"
- Jim Gill, *Jim Gill Sings Moving Rhymes for Modern Times*
- Ella Jenkins, "You'll Sing a Song and I'll Sing a Song"

HANDOUT 9.2 From *Counting Down to Kindergarten: A Complete Guide to Creating a School Readiness Program for Your Community*, R. Lynn Baker (Chicago: American Library Association, 2015).

Week 3: Reading

Reading skills begin before a child can read the words on the page. Reading together increases vocabulary. If you read twenty minutes per day with your child, he or she will be exposed to 1.8 million words of text every year!

How to help your child now:

- Create a reading area for your child to spend time alone with books. This helps develop a love of reading and awareness of printed words.
- Read stories in an interactive way. Ask questions that ask more than just yes-or-no questions as you go through the story. Ask your child what he or she thinks will happen next or questions about the illustrations.
- Read books about kindergarten. If your child is anxious about going to school, books with characters who are also going through the same emotions help children cope with their feelings.
- Let your child see you reading. What is important to you becomes what is important to children. If you enjoy it, they will, too.

Studies show that reading with your child for twenty minutes a day increases the likelihood that your child will be a successful reader later in school.

How to help your child now:

- Set aside a special time to read together every day.
- Go to the library and choose books together.
- Read the same book together more than one time—children learn through repetition. Read the book in a different way each time to keep it enjoyable. Try just talking about the pictures on the page one time, or try singing the words together to a familiar tune.

Books that encourage early reading skills:

- *Brown Bear, Brown Bear, What Do You See?* by Bill Martin Jr. (illus. by Eric Carle)
- *We Are in a Book* by Mo Willems
- *Is Everyone Ready for Fun?* by Jan Thomas
- *Bear Snores On* by Karma Wilson
- *The Little Mouse, the Red Ripe Strawberry, and the Big Hungry Bear* by Don Wood

HANDOUT 9.3 From *Counting Down to Kindergarten: A Complete Guide to Creating a School Readiness Program for Your Community,* R. Lynn Baker (Chicago: American Library Association, 2015).

Week 4: Writing

Studies show that early childhood writing skills, such as drawing and a child writing his or her own name, has a strong connection to reading success later.

How to help your child now:

- Supply lots of different types of writing instruments at home (pencils, pens, markers, colored pencils, crayons).
- Encourage your child to help you write your grocery list—you can even have them write their own short list and draw pictures of the items on their list.
- Play restaurant at home and encourage your child to write down (or draw) your order.
- Help your child practice writing his or her name by using a highlighter to write it on lined paper. Encourage your child to trace over the highlighter.

There is a connection between hand strength and writing skills.

How to help your child now:

- Doodling, scribbling, and drawing are all great ways for your child to strengthen the hand muscles needed for writing.
- Give your child some plastic tweezers and ask him or her to pick up small items with them (such as cotton balls). This will help your child build the hand strength needed for holding a pencil.
- Playing with blocks such as Legos helps your child build hand strength.

Books that encourage writing and writing awareness:

- *Rocket Writes a Story* by Tad Hills
- *Scribbles and Ink* by Ethan Long
- *The Pencil* by Allan Ahlberg
- The Library Mouse series by Daniel Kirk

HANDOUT 9.4 From *Counting Down to Kindergarten: A Complete Guide to Creating a School Readiness Program for Your Community,* R. Lynn Baker (Chicago: American Library Association, 2015).

Week 5: Playing

Studies show that play can connect to all areas of development, including the development of reading skills.

How to help your child now:

- Play together with your child. Incorporate printed text into your play as much as possible.
- Engage in dramatic play that encourages your child to write, such as playing restaurant or post office.
- Take your child to play with other children their age. Register them for library programs—as well as other programs in the community—with their peers.

There is a connection between playing and a successful transition into kindergarten.

How to help your child now:

- Model taking turns and sharing for your child at home and with other children.
- Take your child to the park and encourage them to make friends with other children there.
- Play board games with your child that work on taking turns, following directions, sharing, and even sometimes losing. It is important to show your child that following directions is important.

Books about play:

- *What about Bear?* by Suzanne Bloom
- *Let's Do Nothing!* by Tony Fucile
- *Can You Make a Scary Face?* by Jan Thomas
- *Llama Llama Time to Share* by Anna Dewdney

HANDOUT 9.5 From *Counting Down to Kindergarten: A Complete Guide to Creating a School Readiness Program for Your Community,* R. Lynn Baker (Chicago: American Library Association, 2015).

Week 6:
Self-Help and Motor Skills

Studies show that most kindergarten teachers see self-help and motor skills as two of the most important skills for making a successful transition into kindergarten.

How to help your child now:

- Work on activities that encourage your child to take care of his or her needs at home, including bathroom needs, eating needs, and taking care of clothing.
- Be positive with your child as he or she works to master skills. Encourage rather than correct your child.
- Find fun ways to excite your child about books and writing. Create opportunities to work on these skills as part of play.

There is a connection between self-help and motor skills.

How to help your child now:

- Children who have more-developed motor skills will be better able to take care of their own needs.
- Provide assistance only when needed when your child gets dressed each day. Encourage your child to try to do what he or she can without assistance.
- Encourage your child to hang up his or her jacket, and give your child chores around that the house in order to model personal responsibility.

Books about self-help and motor skills:

- *How Do Dinosaurs Clean Their Room?* by Jane Yolen
- *Ella Sarah Gets Dressed* by Margaret Chodos-Irvine
- *The Kissing Hand* by Audrey Penn
- *The Night before Kindergarten* by Natasha Wing

HANDOUT 9.6 From *Counting Down to Kindergarten: A Complete Guide to Creating a School Readiness Program for Your Community,* R. Lynn Baker (Chicago: American Library Association, 2015).

Index

f denotes figures